Space Science

ROCKY PLANETS

How to use this book

Welcome to *Space Science*. All the books in this set are organized to help you through the multitude of pictures and facts that make this subject so interesting. There is also a master glossary for the set on pages 58–64 and an index on pages 65–72.

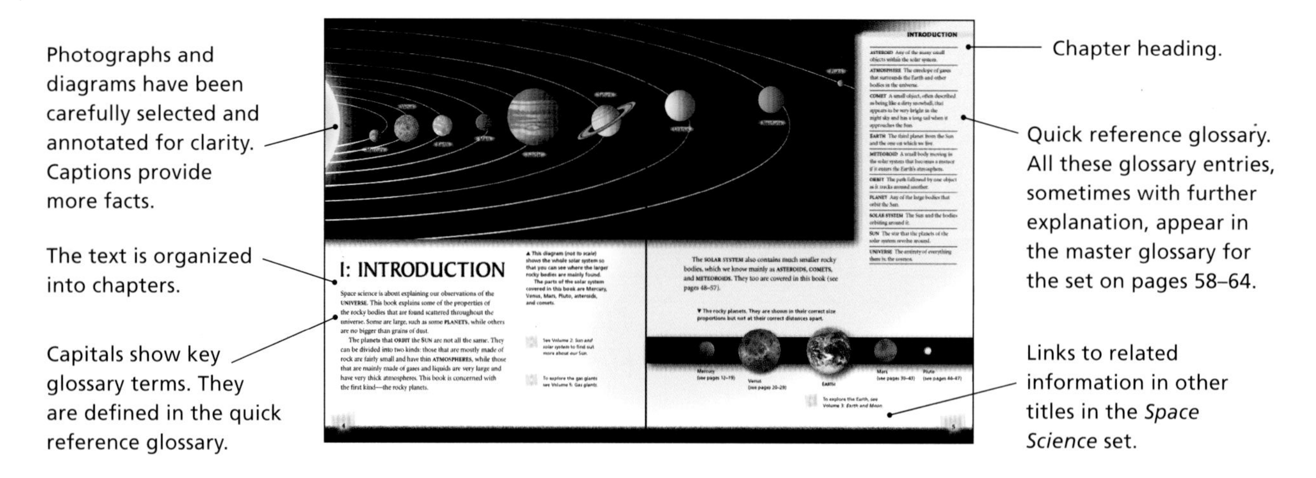

Grolier

First published in the United States in 2004 by Grolier, a division of Scholastic Library Publishing, Sherman Turnpike, Danbury, CT 06816

Author
Brian Knapp, BSc, PhD

Art Director
Duncan McCrae, BSc

Senior Designer
Adele Humphries, BA, PGCE

Editors
Mary Sanders, BSc, and Gillian Gatehouse

Illustrations on behalf of Earthscape Editions
David Woodroffe and David Hardy

Design and production
EARTHSCAPE EDITIONS

Print
WKT Company Limited, Hong Kong

This product is manufactured from sustainable managed forests. For every tree cut down, at least one more is planted.

Library of Congress Cataloging-in-Publication Data
Space science.
p. cm.
Includes index.
Summary: An exploration of the planet Earth, the Moon, solar system, and universe.
Contents: v. 1. How the universe works—v. 2. Sun and solar system—v. 3. Earth and Moon—v. 4. Rocky planets—v. 5. Gas giants—v. 6. Journey into space—v. 7. Shuttle to Space Station —v. 8. What satellites see.
ISBN 0-7172-5825-4 (set : alk. paper)—ISBN 0-7172-5826-2 (v. 1 : alk. paper)—ISBN 0-7172-5827-0 (v. 2 : alk. paper)—ISBN 0-7172-5828-9 (v. 3 : alk. paper)—ISBN 0-7172-5829-7 (v. 4 : alk. paper)—ISBN 0-7172-5830-0 (v. 5 : alk. paper)—ISBN 0-7172-5831-9 (v. 6 : alk. paper)—ISBN 0-7172-5832-7 (v. 7 : alk. paper)—ISBN 0-7172-5833-5 (v. 8 : alk. paper).
1. Space sciences—Juvenile literature. [1. Space sciences.] Grolier Incorporated.
QB500.22.S65 2004
500.5—dc22
2003061836

Picture credits
All photographs and diagrams NASA except the following:
(c=center t=top b=bottom l=left r=right)

Earthscape Editions 4–5t, 7, 19, 29, 43, 44b, 48b, 52t; *John Hopkins University Applied Physics Laboratory/Southwest Research Institute (JHUAPL/SwRI)* 56; *NASA* and *G Bacon* 47; *NASA Artist D. Seal* 12, 24, 30t, 46, 49, 54t.

The front cover shows the planet Venus; the back cover, the rocky surface of Mars.

NASA, the U.S. National Aeronautics and Space Administration, was founded in 1958 for aeronautical and space exploration. It operates several installations around the country and has its headquarters in Washington, D.C.

CONTENTS

▲ Mars in false color.

▲ This diagram (*not to scale*) shows the whole solar system so that you can see where the larger rocky bodies are mainly found.

The parts of the solar system covered in this book are Mercury, Venus, Mars, Pluto, asteroids, and comets.

1: INTRODUCTION

Space science is about explaining our observations of the **UNIVERSE.** This book explains some of the properties of the rocky bodies that are found scattered throughout the universe. Some are large, such as some **PLANETS**, while others are no bigger than grains of dust.

The planets that **ORBIT** the **SUN** are not all the same. They can be divided into two kinds: those that are mostly made of rock are fairly small and have thin **ATMOSPHERES**, while those that are mainly made of gases and liquids are very large and have very thick atmospheres. This book is concerned with the first kind—the rocky planets.

See Volume 2: *Sun and solar system* to find out more about our Sun.

To explore the gas giants, see Volume 5: *Gas giants*.

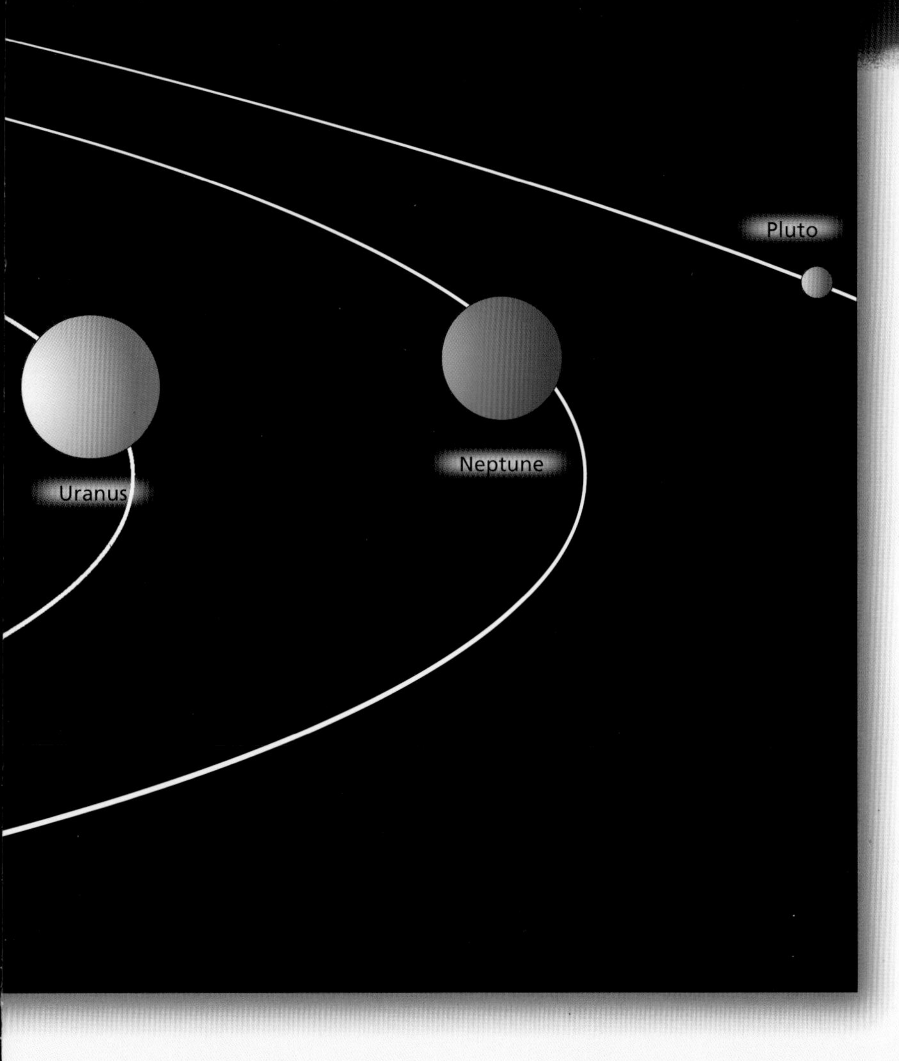

ASTEROID Any of the many small objects within the solar system.

ATMOSPHERE The envelope of gases that surrounds the Earth and other bodies in the universe.

COMET A small object, often described as being like a dirty snowball, that appears to be very bright in the night sky and has a long tail when it approaches the Sun.

EARTH The third planet from the Sun and the one on which we live.

METEOROID A small body moving in the solar system that becomes a meteor if it enters the Earth's atmosphere.

ORBIT The path followed by one object as it tracks around another.

PLANET Any of the large bodies that orbit the Sun.

SOLAR SYSTEM The Sun and the bodies orbiting around it.

SUN The star that the planets of the solar system revolve around.

UNIVERSE The entirety of everything there is; the cosmos.

The **SOLAR SYSTEM** also contains much smaller rocky bodies, which we know mainly as **ASTEROIDS, COMETS,** and **METEOROIDS.** They too are covered in this book (see pages 48–57).

▼ The rocky planets. They are shown in their correct size proportions but not at their correct distances apart.

Mercury
(see pages 12–19)

Venus
(see pages 20–29)

EARTH

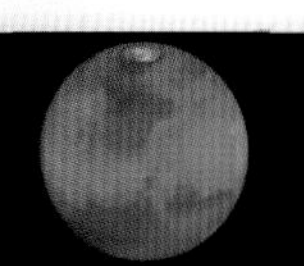

Mars
(see pages 30–43)

Pluto
(see pages 44–47)

To explore the Earth, see Volume 3: *Earth and Moon.*

▲ A view from Earth's **LIMB** during sunrise with Mars and Venus rising.

See Volume 1: *How the universe works* for more information on stars.

Discovery of rocky bodies

When ancient peoples looked from the Earth to the heavens at night, they saw not only the **MOON** but also a multitude of other bright objects. Not only could they see twinkling **STARS**, but they could also detect bright objects in the sky that did not twinkle. They included Venus, Mars, and Mercury, together with **COMETS** and **METEOROIDS** (shooting stars).

Venus was first observed by the Babylonians 5,000 years ago as a brilliant white "evening star." Mercury was also seen both as an evening star and as a "morning star." Mars, too, is easily found in the night sky, not as a brilliant white planet but as a blood-red planet—full of menace, or so it seemed.

As the ancients studied the night sky, they became aware that it was generally a very constant and predictable place, its stars and other bodies moving with orderly, slow motions as seen from the Earth. But comets were different. They appeared suddenly, moved quickly across the sky, and then disappeared. Complete with white tail, they were believed to be a sign that something important (good or bad) was about to happen.

Much smaller and more often seen on clear nights were tiny sparks of light that darted across the sky, often numbering hundreds an hour. These "shooting stars" are meteoroids, fragments of rock that cross the path of the Earth as it travels through space.

▲ This iron **METEORITE** was found in Antarctica and is mostly made of iron and nickel. This sample is probably a small piece from the core of a large **ASTEROID** that broke up.

All of these rocky objects could be seen from Earth with the naked eye. Pluto, the furthermost rocky body in the solar system, however, was different. It was completely unknown to people on Earth until the 20th century because it was too far away and too small to be seen even with powerful telescopes. Pluto had to be discovered by science.

What the rocky planets have in common

The planets orbit the Sun in very regular ways separated by enormous distances in which there is very little **MATTER** at all.

The planets all lie in the same **PLANE**—that is, if looked at from the level of their orbits, the planets all appear to be more or less in a straight line centered on the Sun. The planets also all revolve in the same direction as the Sun.

Because of this arrangement it is as though they were all formed from the same flat **DISK** of material, or **NEBULA.** Astronomers think this happened over four billion years ago.

The inner planets—Mercury, Venus, Earth, and Mars—are fairly close to the Sun. All alone and far out on the edge of the solar system lies Pluto (although there is still much controversy about exactly what Pluto is made of, and it may have much in common with comets).

Venus, Earth, and Mars all have orbits that are nearly circular; but the orbits of Mercury and Pluto are very elliptical (or oval-shaped).

ASTEROID Any of the many small objects within the solar system.

COMET A small object, often described as being like a dirty snowball, that appears to be very bright in the night sky and has a long tail when it approaches the Sun.

DISK A shape or surface that looks round and flat.

LIMB The outer edge of a celestial body, including an atmosphere if it has one.

MATTER Anything that exists in physical form.

METEORITE A meteor that reaches the Earth's surface.

METEOROID A small body moving in the solar system that becomes a meteor if it enters the Earth's atmosphere.

MOON The natural satellite that orbits the Earth.

NEBULA (pl. **NEBULAE**) Clouds of gas and dust that exist in the space between stars.

PLANE A flat surface.

STAR A large ball of gases that radiates light. The star nearest the Earth is the Sun.

▼ This diagram shows the orbits of the four rocky planet neighbors. Together they form the group of inner planets.

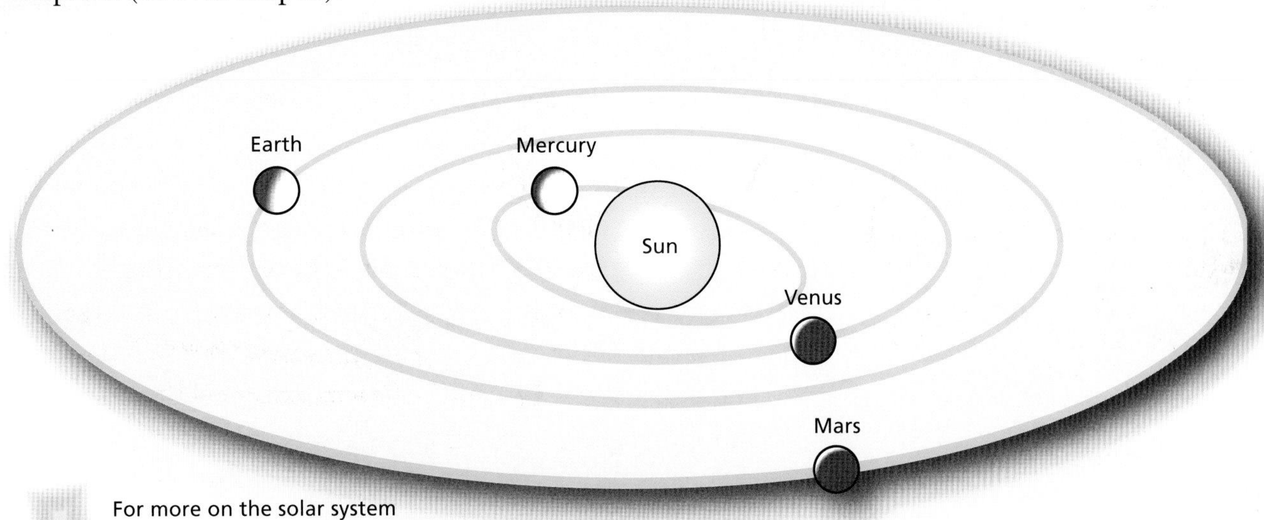

For more on the solar system
see Volume 2: *Sun and solar system*.

A unique history

The rocky planets are made mostly of the ELEMENTS iron, silicon, and oxygen. This is not the same composition as the universe, so they must have experienced a history that removed many of the common elements (such as hydrogen and helium) and left concentrations of those elements we see today.

Whatever the special planet-forming process was, it probably occurred because SPACE became gradually colder. As a result, some elements with high BOILING POINTS stopped drifting around as gases and became liquids and then solids.

The process by which this happens can be seen around us all the time. It is called CONDENSATION, and it happens, for example, whenever WATER VAPOR condenses to liquid water or to ice.

Pluto does not seem to fit into this scheme. It is not only very much smaller than the other planets, it is perhaps best thought of as being more like a comet than a planet in composition, since it is a mixture of rock and ice.

Moons

The rocky planets are each single bodies of matter. Earth and Mars have moons (large SATELLITES) that rotate around them, but they do not have the bands of dust and the numerous moons that are so common in the JOVIAN PLANETS.

The moons of the rocky planets have nearly circular orbits that lie in the same plane as the EQUATOR of their parent planets. They all also revolve in the same direction as their planets. In this sense the moons behave in the same way with respect to their parents as the planets do to the Sun.

For more on our Moon see Volume 3: *Earth and Moon*.

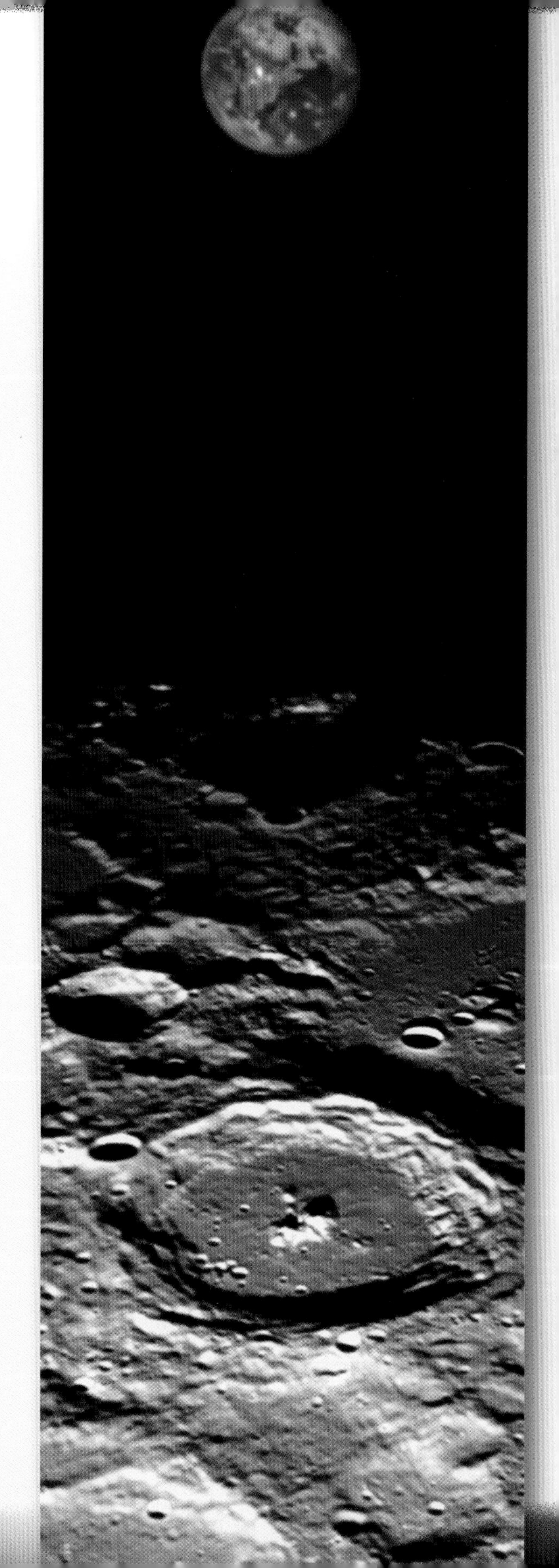

▶ The rocky Earth as seen from its rocky satellite, the Moon.

▲ The cratered terrain of Mercury.

Craters

Of the rocky planets and their moons, two of them—Mercury and our Moon—show massive **CRATERS** covering their surfaces.

Because Mercury and the Moon have hardly any atmospheres and appear to be internally almost inactive, their surfaces probably still look much as they did in the early stages of the formation of the solar system.

Elsewhere, either the craters are hidden below swirling clouds of atmosphere, or internal (geological) changes have altered them, so that all but the most recent are less visible. For example, research has also shown such craters in the surface rocks of the Earth.

As a result, it seems quite likely that at the beginning of the life of the planets, they gained material from the bombardment of space debris in the form of asteroids and meteoroids hitting them. This is still happening (as shown, for example, by Meteor Crater in Arizona, see page 52), but at a dramatically slower rate compared with the early history of the planets.

BOILING POINT The change of state of a substance in which a liquid rapidly turns into a gas without a change in temperature.

CONDENSATION The change of state from a gas or vapor to a liquid.

CRATER A deep bowl-shaped depression in the surface of a body formed by the high-speed impact of another, smaller body.

ELEMENT A substance that cannot be decomposed into simpler substances by chemical means.

EQUATOR The ring drawn around a body midway between the poles.

JOVIAN PLANETS An alternative group name for the gas giant planets: Jupiter, Saturn, Uranus, and Neptune.

SATELLITE An object that is in an orbit around another object, usually a planet.

SPACE Everything beyond the Earth's atmosphere.

WATER VAPOR The gaseous form of water. Also sometimes referred to as moisture.

The small rock fragments

As well as large rocky bodies, our solar system also contains an incalculable number of small fragments of rock. We call them **ASTEROIDS**, **COMETS**, **METEOROIDS**, and **INTERPLANETARY DUST**. The compositions of all but the comets are similar to the rocky planets.

Asteroids are the biggest in this category. Often called minor planets, they can be several hundred kilometers across. Some, for example, Ceres, Pallas, and Vesta, are substantial enough to have names. Most, however, are less than 10 km across.

Asteroids are all located in the same place because that is where they are stable. If they were anywhere else, they would be affected by the **GRAVITY** of the planets and be attracted to one of them.

It is likely that the early solar system had asteroids scattered all over it, with orbits in many directions around the Sun. But the bigger planets probably swept up most of them as their paths crossed. Only those that had orbits similar to those of the planets survived.

▲ The asteroid Gaspra has a surface covered with "soil" and rocks that are a pale gray, paler than those on Earth's Moon.

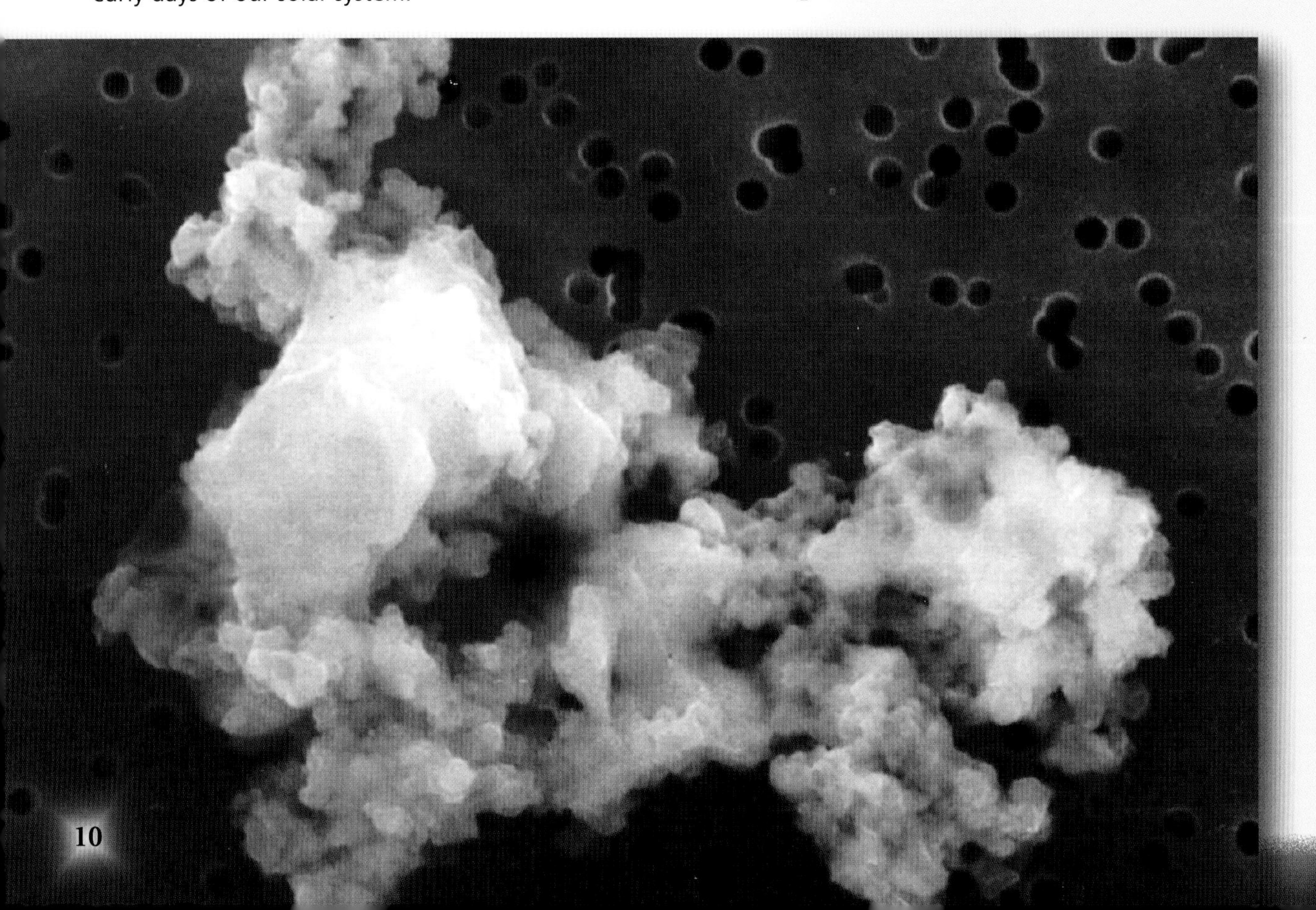

▼ This is "stardust," an interplanetary dust fragment made of glass, carbon, and silicate **MINERAL** grains. It measures only 10 **MICRONS** across (a tenth of the width of a typical human hair). This piece of dust most likely originates from the early days of our solar system.

▲ This meteorite—a material called chondrite—was collected from Antarctica. It is thought to have formed at the same time as the planets in the solar system, about 4.55 billion years ago.

You can see this process today because, when stray bits of space rock—called meteoroids—cross the path of the Earth, they enter the atmosphere and heat up, starting to glow. They are then called **METEORS**, or shooting stars. Any debris that manages to arrive on the surface before it burns up is called a **METEORITE** (see pages 55 and 57).

When meteorites are examined, they are found to have an age close to that of the formation of the solar system. It may well be that they are the leftover remains of the building blocks, or **PLANETESIMALS**, from which the major planets began to form.

Asteroids are irregular in shape, suggesting that they have formed by being shattered after violent collisions. So they may just be the remains of former small planets that collided so violently that they smashed themselves apart instead of combining to make an even larger planet. Because they are small, their internal gravity is not strong enough to mold them into **SPHERES**.

The smallest fragments and dust are probably the debris left over after collisions between asteroids and comets. Some people refer to them as "stardust."

ASTEROID Any of the many small objects within the solar system.

COMET A small object, often described as being like a dirty snowball, that appears to be very bright in the night sky and has a long tail when it approaches the Sun.

GRAVITY The force of attraction between bodies.

INTERPLANETARY DUST The fine dustlike material that lies scattered through space, and that exists between the planets as well as in outer space.

METEOR A streak of light (shooting star) produced by a meteoroid as it enters the Earth's atmosphere.

METEORITE A meteor that reaches the Earth's surface.

METEOROID A small body moving in the solar system that becomes a meteor if it enters the Earth's atmosphere.

MICRON A millionth of a meter.

MINERAL A solid crystalline substance.

PLANETESIMAL Small rocky bodies one kilometer to hundreds of kilometers across.

SPHERE A ball-shaped object.

2: MERCURY

Mercury (which is just 4,878 km across) is the smallest planet in the solar system apart from Pluto and just about the same size as our Moon (although its **GRAVITY** is 2.3 times greater).

Mercury is the closest planet in the solar system to the Sun, following a pronounced elliptical (or oval-shaped) **ORBIT** that varies from 46 million km to 70 million km, an average of 58 million km from the Sun.

Mercury is a rocky planet with a **DENSITY** of 5.4 g/cm^3, similar to that of the Earth. However, since Mercury is smaller, it does not have as large a **GRAVITATIONAL FIELD** as the Earth and so cannot use the same force of gravity to compress the material at its **CORE**. As a result, to have the same density, it must be mainly made of materials that are more dense than those on the Earth. This suggests that proportionally it has a larger iron-rich core and a thinner **CRUST** than the Earth.

CORE The central region of a body.

CRUST The solid outer surface of a rocky body.

DENSITY A measure of the amount of matter in a space.

GRAVITATIONAL FIELD The region surrounding a body in which that body's gravitational force can be felt.

GRAVITY The force of attraction between bodies.

ORBIT The path followed by one object as it tracks around another.

PHOTOMOSAIC A composite picture made up of several other pictures that individually only cover a small area.

PROBE An unmanned spacecraft designed to explore our solar system and beyond.

▼ An artist's impression of the surface of Mercury and space **PROBE** Mariner 10 (see page 14).

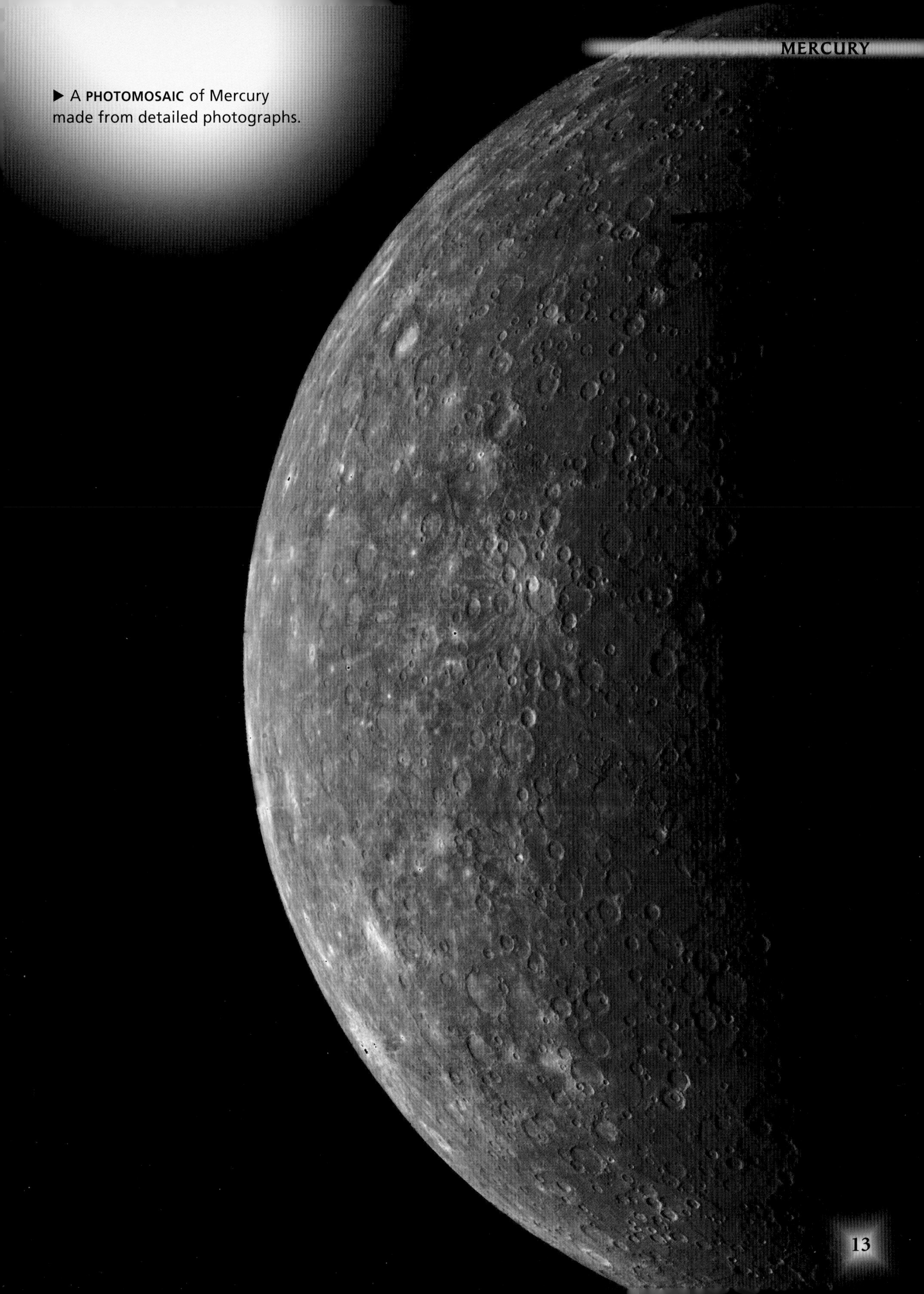

▶ A **PHOTOMOSAIC** of Mercury made from detailed photographs.

Observing Mercury

The planet Mercury is easy to see without a telescope and, because it lies inside the orbit of the Earth, can be found in the sky just before sunrise and just after sunset. Because of its position between us and the Sun Mercury also shows **PHASES** like the Moon, changing from a thin crescent to a full **DISK**. At the same time, because Mercury is close to the Sun, it is difficult to get good images of it from ground-based telescopes. All the closeup pictures of Mercury come from the Mariner 10 spaceflights.

Because of its orbit, close to the Earth and yet inside the Earth's orbit, the size of Mercury appears to change (as does Venus) as it completes an orbit around the Sun.

It is a full disk when it appears on the opposite side of the Sun from the Earth. Since that is also when it is furthest from the Earth, Mercury also then looks its smallest. When it is closest to the Earth, it appears larger, but then only as a thin crescent. Mercury appears to be between $^{1}/_{180}$ and $^{1}/_{380}$ the size of the Moon depending on its position in its orbit relative to the Earth.

For more on the Mariner probes and the slingshot trajectory see "Outer worlds" in Volume 6: *Journey into space*.

Mariner 10

◀ Mariner 10 was the first spacecraft to use the **GRAVITY** of one planet to **ACCELERATE** it, or "slingshot" it, to another (the path taken is called a **SLINGSHOT TRAJECTORY**). Mariner 10 used Venus's gravity to be flung to Mercury.

Mariner 10's orbit crossed Mercury's: the first time at a distance of 703 kilometers from the planet, the second time at 48,069 kilometers, and a third time at 327 kilometers. In total, Mariner 10 imaged about half the planet. Mercury was revealed to have a very cratered, Moonlike surface and a faint, mostly helium atmosphere.

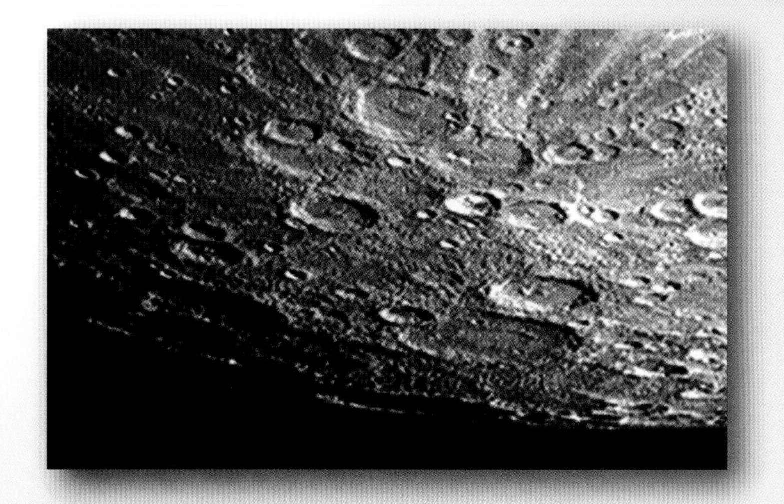

◀ This is a picture of the area near Mercury's south pole taken by Mariner 10 when it was about 83,000 km from the planet.

Rotation and orbit

Mercury orbits the Sun once every 88 Earth days, so that it passes the Earth once every 116 days. This is called the **SYNODIC PERIOD**. By contrast, Mercury spins very slowly, taking nearly 59 Earth days to complete one Mercurial day.

The long daily spin means that it rotates three times on its **AXIS** in the time it takes it to revolve twice around the Sun. So, at the start of the next Mercurial day the Sun is no longer in the same part of the sky. In fact, it takes 176 Earth days or 2 Mercurial years for that to happen.

From the point of view of a person on Mercury's surface the great oval orbit also means that the Sun appears to change size during the year, becoming almost half as big again at its closest point compared to its size at its furthest point.

The atmosphere

Mercury is a small planet, and so its **GRAVITATIONAL PULL** is not large. Because of this it has been relatively easy for many gases to leave the **ATMOSPHERE** of Mercury. At the same time, being so close to the Sun, the surface of Mercury is very hot. That, too, would tend to boil off liquids that would then, as gases, disperse into space. As a result, the wispy air around Mercury is just a five hundred billionth as dense as that on Earth.

ACCELERATE To gain speed.

ATMOSPHERE The envelope of gases that surrounds the Earth and other bodies in the universe.

AXIS (pl. **AXES**) The line around which a body spins.

DISK A shape or surface that looks round and flat.

GRAVITY/GRAVITATIONAL PULL
The force of attraction between bodies. The larger an object, the more its gravitational pull on other objects.

PHASE The differing appearance of a body that is closer to the Sun, and that is illuminated by it.

SLINGSHOT TRAJECTORY A path chosen to use the attractive force of gravity to increase the speed of a spacecraft. The craft is flown toward the planet or star, and it speeds up under the gravitational force. At the correct moment the path is taken to send the spacecraft into orbit and, when pointing in the right direction, to turn it from orbit, with its increased velocity, toward the final destination.

SYNODIC PERIOD The time needed for an object within the solar system, such as a planet, to return to the same place relative to the Sun as seen from the Earth.

The main gases in the Mercurial atmosphere are hydrogen, helium, sodium, potassium, and oxygen.

Both hydrogen and helium are easily lost from the atmospheres of planets (they are in very low amounts in the Earth's atmosphere, for example), so their presence suggests that they are either seeping from within the planet or from material that flows from the Sun and is carried to Mercury by the **SOLAR WIND**.

Such a thin atmosphere can have no possible effect on the materials of the planet's surface, so there are no **SAND DUNES** or other features that might be expected if there were powerful winds. Indeed, the **CRATERS** that cover the surface look untouched.

With no air and no clouds to **REFLECT** the rays from the Sun or hold in any heat that has been absorbed during the day, the planet's surface temperature soars up to 950°C at noon (there is no lag until the hottest time of day as on Earth) and cools down to 373°C just before dawn.

Mercury has no seasons because it does not spin at an angle to its orbit. Instead, its **EQUATOR** lies almost exactly on the **PLANE** of its orbit. The main seasonal effects are due to the fact that Mercury is sometimes much closer to the Sun than at other times in its orbit. In a Mercurial year there are thus two periods of hottest ground surface and two periods when it is cooler.

How Mercury's features are named

The surface of Mercury has only been seen since 1974, and all of the features have been named since then according to these rules: Impact craters are named for famous men and women; **SCARPS** are named for ships used in exploration on Earth; **RIDGES** and **VALLEYS** are named for astronomers and radio observatories; plains use the name of the god Mercury in a number of languages; and mountains other than crater scarps are named for the nearest plains.

Craters

▲ Mariner 10 took this picture of the densely cratered surface of Mercury when the spacecraft was 18,200 kilometers from the planet.

The smaller, fresh crater at the center bottom is about 25 kilometers in diameter.

Scarps

▶ A scarp, or cliff, more than 300 kilometers long extends diagonally from upper left to lower right in the picture.

It is thought to have been formed by the crust contracting around a slightly shrinking core.

The picture was taken from 64,500 kilometers.

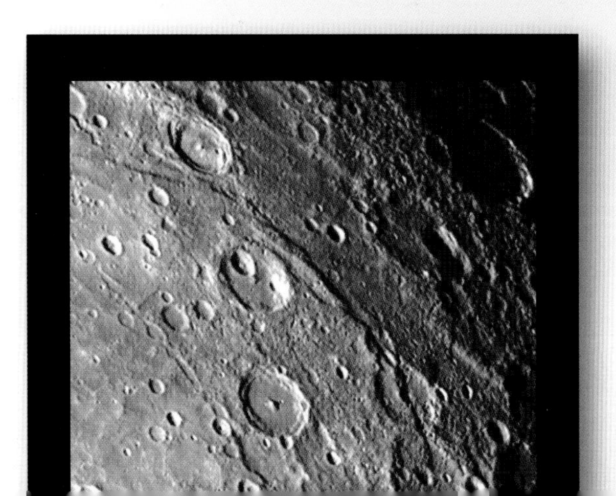

The surface of Mercury

Mercury has a mainly rocky surface with some thin surface dust ("soil") several centimeters thick covering **PLAINS** made by ancient **LAVA FLOWS**. This is quite like our Moon. The color is, however, darker than our Moon, suggesting that the rocks are more iron-rich. There are also two **ICE CAPS**, displaced somewhat from the **POLES** and existing in those areas that are in shadow.

▼ This picture of Mercury shows north at the top. The **LIMB** is at right, as is the illuminating sunlight. The equator crosses the planet about two-thirds of the way from the top of the disk.

The planet shows a **GIBBOUS** disk—more than half illuminated. This hemisphere is dominated by smooth plains and looks like areas of the Moon's **MARIA**. Half of a very large, multiringed **BASIN** named Caloris Basin (see page 18) appears near the center of the disk. Its surrounding mountain ring is 1,300 kilometers in diameter.

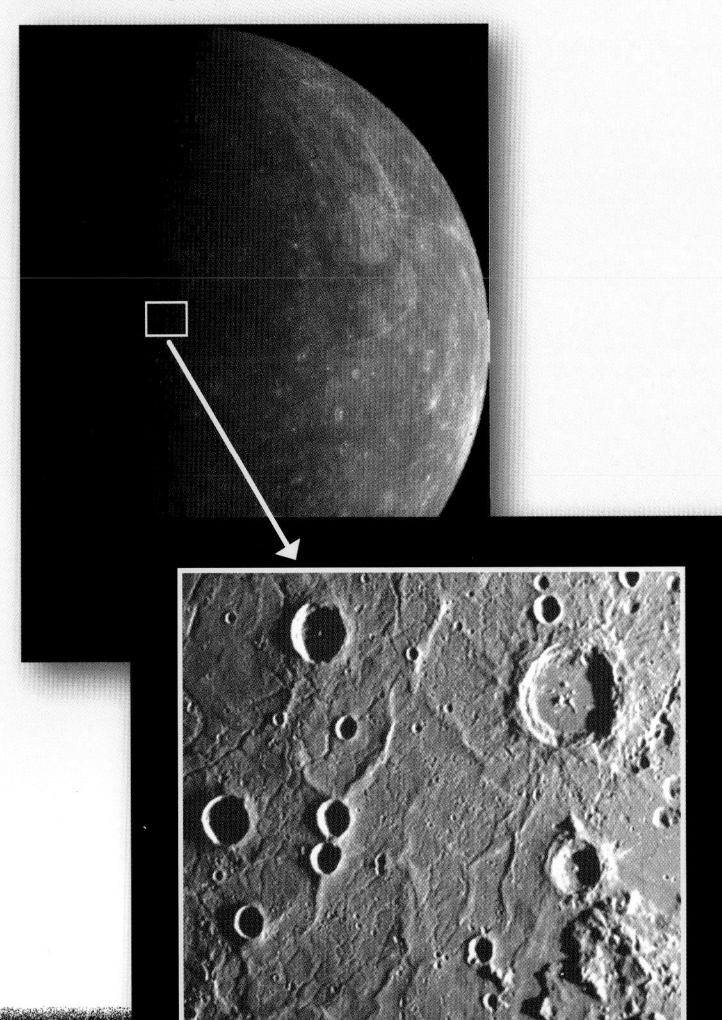

BASIN A large depression in the ground (bigger than a crater).

CRATER A deep bowl-shaped depression in the surface of a body formed by the high-speed impact of another, smaller body.

EQUATOR The ring drawn around a body midway between the poles.

FRACTURE A break in brittle rock.

GIBBOUS When between half and a full disk of a body can be seen lighted by the Sun.

ICE CAP A small mountainous region that is covered in ice.

LAVA FLOW A river or sheet of liquid volcanic rock.

LIMB The outer edge of a celestial body, including an atmosphere if it has one.

MARE (pl. **MARIA**) A flat, dark plain created by lava flows.

PLAIN A flat or gently rolling part of a landscape.

PLANE A flat surface.

POLE The geographic pole is the place where a line drawn along the axis of rotation exits from a body's surface.

REFLECT To bounce back any light that falls on a surface.

RIDGE A narrow crest of an upland area.

SAND DUNE An aerodynamically shaped hump of sand.

SCARP The steep slope of a sharp-crested ridge.

SOLAR WIND The flow of tiny charged particles (called plasma) outward from the Sun.

VALLEY A natural long depression in the landscape.

Ridges and fractures

◀ This shows part of the floor of the Caloris Basin with ridges and **FRACTURES**. Notice that the fractures cut across the ridges at various angles.

Surface features

▲▼ Part of the surface of Mercury shown in FALSE COLOR to enhance some surface features.

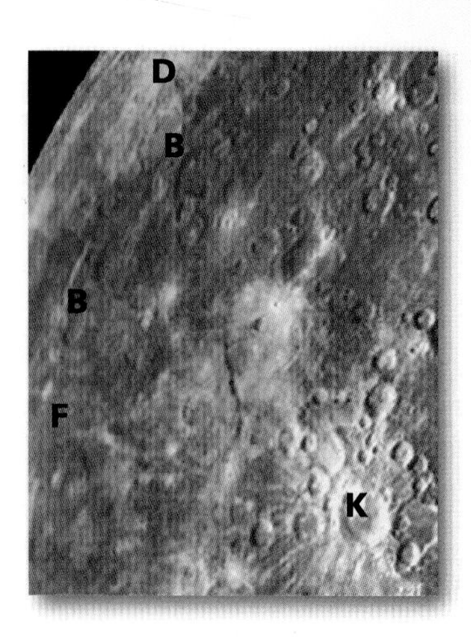

K Material that may have come from below the crust

D Rocky area rich in titanium

B Crust

F Lava flow

It seems, from the enormous number of craters, that Mercury suffered severe bombardment by **METEOROIDS** in the early stages of its history.

The dust is probably produced by the impact of microscopic meteoroids, which are continually hitting the rocky surface because, unlike the Earth, Mercury has no substantial atmosphere in which they would burn up.

The largest surface feature is the Caloris Basin (see page 17), which lies in Mercury's northern hemisphere. It is a large circular **DEPRESSION** about 1,300 km across and was formed by the impact of a large **METEORITE**. The edge of the impact crater forms a ring of mountains up to 2 kilometers high.

Surrounding the craters are circles of land covered in rock fragments. They are the materials scattered from the craters as a result of meteorite collisions. Some blocks thrown from the initial impact landed back on the surface and caused secondary craters. As a result, craters often come in clusters.

However, although the surface seems generally unchanged, there are features that suggest some geological activity. Some of the most prominent are the huge **ESCARPMENTS** that extend for hundreds of kilometers and can be over 3 kilometers high (see bottom picture page 16). The escarpments cut through craters and so must be younger than the craters. They seem to be connected to vertical faults.

With no evidence of any inner **MOLTEN** churning rock to drag the surface around as is the case on Earth, it is likely that these ridges were produced as Mercury has shrunk, possibly as a result of cooling, causing parts of the surface to squash together before one part cracked and overrode another.

Other ridges are often found near craters. They spread out from the craters and probably were produced at the same time as the craters formed, and so are impact features (see bottom picture page 17).

Some areas are not heavily cratered. Here the land surface is made of plains. Plains must be an active feature because otherwise impacts from meteorites would have covered them with craters.

The most likely source of material to cover over, or resurface, some areas is **LAVA** and **ASH**. But even the plains show small craters, suggesting that they were formed after the main period of meteorite activity but, nevertheless, a long time ago.

Inside Mercury

The fact that Mercury is, on average, a dense planet suggests that a large part of it must be made of a dense material such as a **COMPOUND** of iron. The iron core may be about 1,900 km in **RADIUS**. If that is so, then that only leaves about 500 km of surface crust and **MANTLE** to enclose it.

Mercury has a weak **MAGNETIC FIELD**. For a magnetic field to form, there has to be a region of moving molten material, suggesting that the outer part of the core is probably molten. However, because the field is very weak, it may be that the rocks of the core are no longer moving, but that all of the **MAGNETISM** is due to rocks that were magnetized during an early period when part of the core was molten (much as a permanent magnet holds its magnetism when the source of magnetism is removed).

ASH Fragments of lava that have cooled and solidified between when they leave a volcano and when they fall to the surface.

COMPOUND A substance made from two or more elements that have chemically combined.

DEPRESSION A sunken area or hollow in a surface or landscape.

ESCARPMENT A sharp-edged ridge.

FALSE COLOR The colors used to make the appearance of some property more obvious.

LAVA Hot, melted rock from a volcano.

MAGNETIC FIELD The region of influence of a magnetic body.

MAGNETISM An invisible force that has the property of attracting iron and similar metals.

MANTLE The region of a planet between the core and the crust.

METEORITE A meteor that reaches the Earth's surface.

METEOROID A small body moving in the solar system that becomes a meteor if it enters the Earth's atmosphere.

MOLTEN Liquid, suggesting that it has changed from a solid.

RADIUS (pl. **RADII**) The distance from the center to the outside of a circle or sphere.

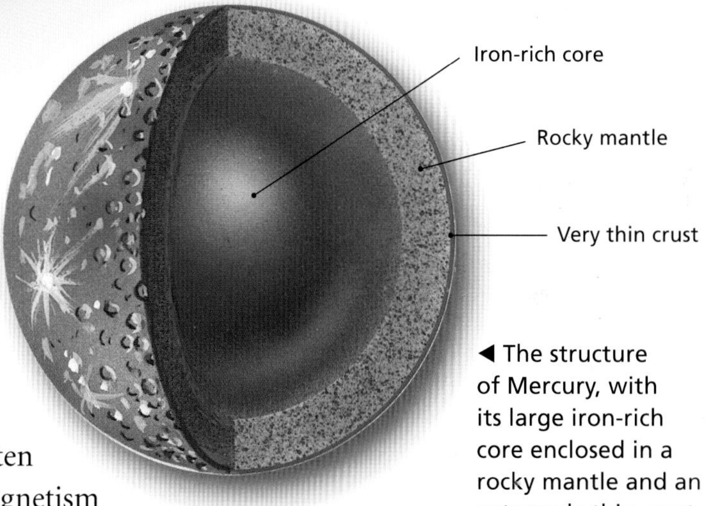

Iron-rich core

Rocky mantle

Very thin crust

◀ The structure of Mercury, with its large iron-rich core enclosed in a rocky mantle and an extremely thin crust.

3: VENUS

Venus is the second planet from the Sun and our closest neighbor.

Venus orbits at an average of 108 million km from the Sun. But because Venus and the Earth have different **ORBITS**, its distance from the Earth varies from 42 million km to 257 million km. As a result, its apparent brightness and size in the sky also change. In fact, Venus has an almost perfectly circular orbit around the Sun, producing a Venusian year of nearly 225 Earth days.

Venus spins on its **AXIS** very slowly, taking 243 Earth days to complete a Venusian day. Venus also spins in the opposite direction from the Earth (called a **RETROGRADE DIRECTION**), so that the Sun rises in the west and sets in the east.

ATMOSPHERE The envelope of gases that surrounds the Earth and other bodies in the universe.

AXIS (pl. **AXES**) The line around which a body spins.

GALILEO A U.S. space probe launched in October 1989 and designed for intensive investigation of Jupiter.

ORBIT The path followed by one object as it tracks around another.

RADAR Short for radio detecting and ranging. A system of bouncing radio waves from objects in order to map their surfaces and find out how far away they are.

RETROGRADE DIRECTION An orbit the opposite of normal—that is, a planet that spins so the Sun rises in the west and sinks in the east.

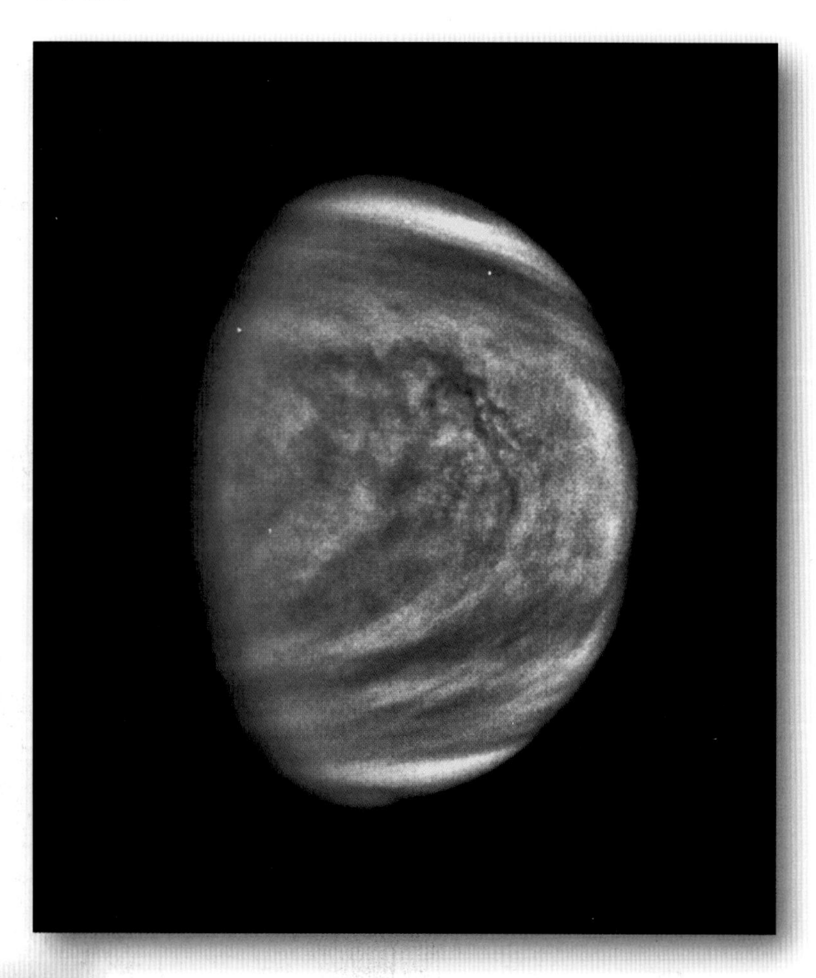

◀ This picture of Venus was taken by the **GALILEO** spacecraft at a range of almost 2.7 million kilometers from the planet. The clouds are made not of water droplets but of droplets of sulfuric acid. The pattern of clouds hints that the **ATMOSPHERE** might change in a way similar to that of the Earth.

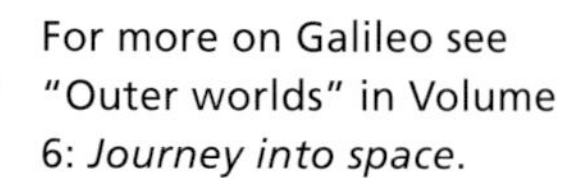

For more on Galileo see "Outer worlds" in Volume 6: *Journey into space*.

▶ The surface of Venus as seen by **RADAR**, which can penetrate the clouds that cloak the surface. That is why this view seems so different from the blue–white image taken in visible light shown on the left.

This global view of the surface of Venus is centered at 180°E longitude.

Radar is described in detail in Volume 8: *What satellites see*.

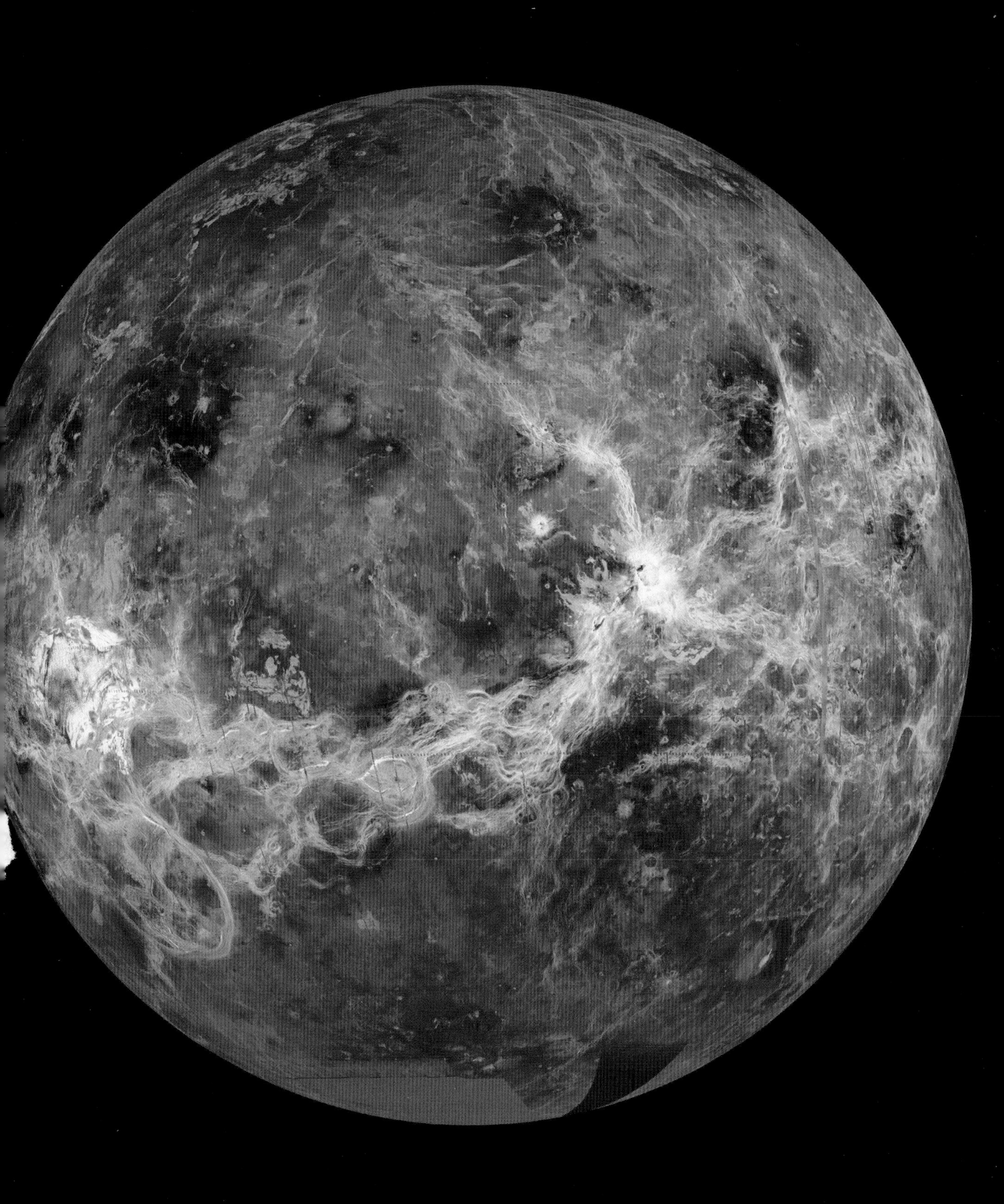

▲ Venus as seen through the Earth's **LIMB**.

We always see the same side of Venus from Earth when Venus and the Earth are closest because of the way the orbits happen to be synchronized (**SYNCHRONOUS ROTATION**).

Like Mercury, Venus lies within the orbit of the Earth and so is seen in **PHASES**, like the Moon.

Venus is also remarkably similar to the Earth in size and **MASS**. Venus is 12,102 km across, which is 95% of the diameter of the Earth, and its mass is just over 81% of the Earth. Its **DENSITY** is just a little lower at 5.2 g/cm^3, compared to 5.5 g/cm^3 for the Earth. However, while the Earth is flattened at the **POLES** due to **CENTRIFUGAL FORCE** pulling out the **EQUATOR** as a result of its fairly fast **ROTATION**, the very slow rotation of Venus means that centrifugal force is not powerful enough to pull out the equatorial rocks. So Venus is a nearly perfect **SPHERE**.

Venus does not have a **MAGNETIC FIELD**, suggesting that there is no movement of **MOLTEN** rock inside the planet. This may be due to the slow rotation of the planet, since magnetic fields appear to be produced by planets that spin quickly.

The magnetic field of a planet normally holds the **SOLAR WIND** at bay; but because Venus has no magnetic field, the solar wind and its particles reach right to the top of the clouds.

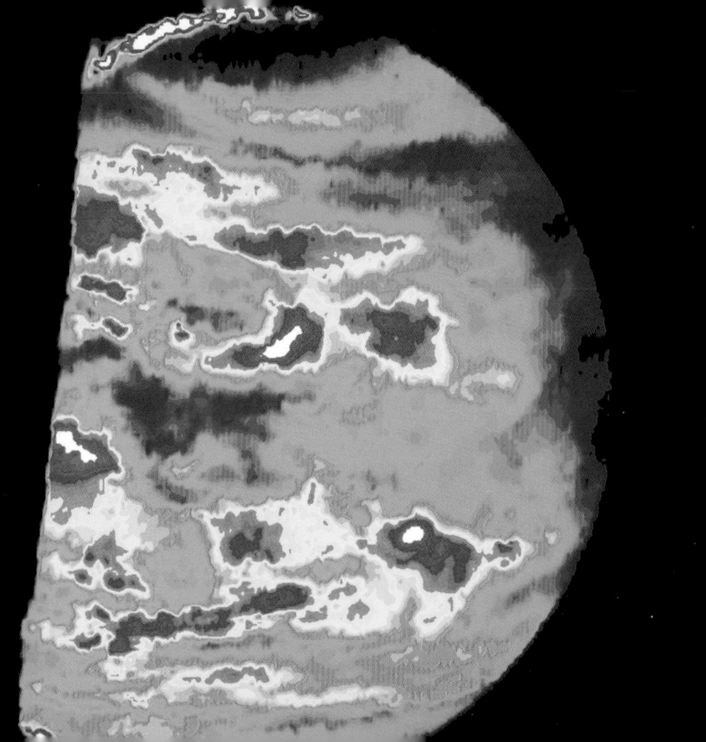

MOLTEN Liquid, suggesting that it has changed from a solid.

PHASE The differing appearance of a body that is closer to the Sun, and that is illuminated by it.

POLE The geographic pole is the place where a line drawn along the axis of rotation exits from a body's surface.

PRESSURE The force per unit area.

ROTATION Spinning around an axis.

SOLAR WIND The flow of tiny charged particles (called plasma) outward from the Sun.

SPHERE A ball-shaped object.

SYNCHRONOUS ROTATION When two bodies make a complete rotation on their axes in the same time.

On the other hand, the carbon dioxide content of the atmosphere produces something like an extreme **GREENHOUSE EFFECT** on Earth. The carbon dioxide traps a large part of the outgoing **RADIATION** from the planet. Furthermore, the clouds reflect another substantial part of the heat trying to leave the planet. The combined effect is to make the surface temperature 1,000°C, high enough to melt lead.

The surface of Venus

We cannot see the surface of Venus directly because of the perpetual shroud of cloud. What we know about the planet therefore comes from using methods for seeing through the cloud. The most important of them has been **RADAR** (see pages 20–21)

The surface of Venus—if we could see it—would seem orangy. That, in part, is due to the filtering effect of the clouds, which tend to let through only the yellowy-white light. As a result, brown rock, such as we would find on the Moon, appears to be orange. The true color of the Venusian surface is thus probably brown.

Using radar, we can detect some very prominent **RIDGES** and mountains. They are called Alpha Regio, Beta Regio, and the Maxwell Montes.

Venus is surprising in that it does not have an entirely cratered surface but one made of gently rolling plains covered in a veneer of stones and a thin layer of dust ("soil"). The rocks appear to be similar in composition to the basalt **LAVA** we have on Earth, suggesting a volcanic origin for the surface. Basalt weathers (ages) from the black color seen soon after it solidifies to a dark brown.

GREENHOUSE EFFECT The increase in atmospheric temperature produced by the presence of carbon dioxide in the air.

LAVA Hot, melted rock from a volcano. Lava flows onto the surface of a planet and cools and hardens to form new rock.

PROBE An unmanned spacecraft designed to explore our solar system and beyond.

RADAR Short for radio detecting and ranging. A system of bouncing radio waves from objects in order to map their surfaces and find out how far away they are.

RADIATION The transfer of energy in the form of waves (such as light and heat) or particles (such as from radioactive decay of a material).

REFLECT To bounce back any light that falls on a surface.

RIDGE A narrow crest of an upland area.

SAND DUNE An aerodynamically shaped hump of sand.

SOLAR RADIATION The light and heat energy sent into space from the Sun.

Magellan

▶ The Magellan spacecraft was named for the Portuguese explorer who first sailed all the way around the Earth. The **PROBE** was designed to develop an understanding of the geological structure of Venus. During its 4-year operation (between 1990 and 1994) it provided detailed maps of Venus's surface using radar to penetrate the planet's thick cloud cover. The radar imaged 98% of the surface, seeing things as small as 100 m across.

Faults and rifts

Among the plains there are some large **BASINS** and also some large areas of high **PLATEAUS**. Furthermore, there are a few long **MOUNTAIN RANGES**. The Maxwell Montes, for example, are more than 10 kilometers high, similar to the height of the Himalayas on Earth.

The pattern of these mountain ranges and their **VALLEYS** suggests that they were formed like those on Earth, that is, by rocks being squashed as **PLATES** collided. Of course, since there is no water on Venus, these mountain ranges have never been subject to water or glacier erosion and stand up just as they were produced.

When plates on the surface of a planet move around, some areas get squashed into mountains, while the opposite sides of the plates pull apart, producing **RIFT VALLEYS**. Often such rifts appear on broad rises formed by the upwelling of **MAGMA** from great depth. This is the case on Earth, but the majority of rises are deep below the oceans. It is best, therefore, to compare the surface of Venus, which has no water, with areas like the East African rift valleys, which are set in a broad dome.

▶ This is a computer-generated view of Latona Corona and Dali Chasma on Venus.

Latona Corona is a circular feature approximately 1,000 kilometers in diameter whose eastern half is shown at the left of the image. It has a relatively smooth, raised rim. Bright lines or **FRACTURES** within the corona appear to radiate away from its center toward the rim.

The rest of the bright fractures in the area are associated with the relatively deep (approximately 3 kilometers) troughs of Dali Chasma, which are very distinct features on Venus.

The broad, curving **SCARP** may be where one part of the crust has been pushed up over another part.

▼ A 3D model of what a Venusian **CHASM** may look like.

The lowlands to the right are made up of overlapping, relatively dark and smooth **LAVA FLOWS**, but the highlands consist mainly of fractures and ridges.

Rift valleys, like the one that crosses the center of the image, are common.

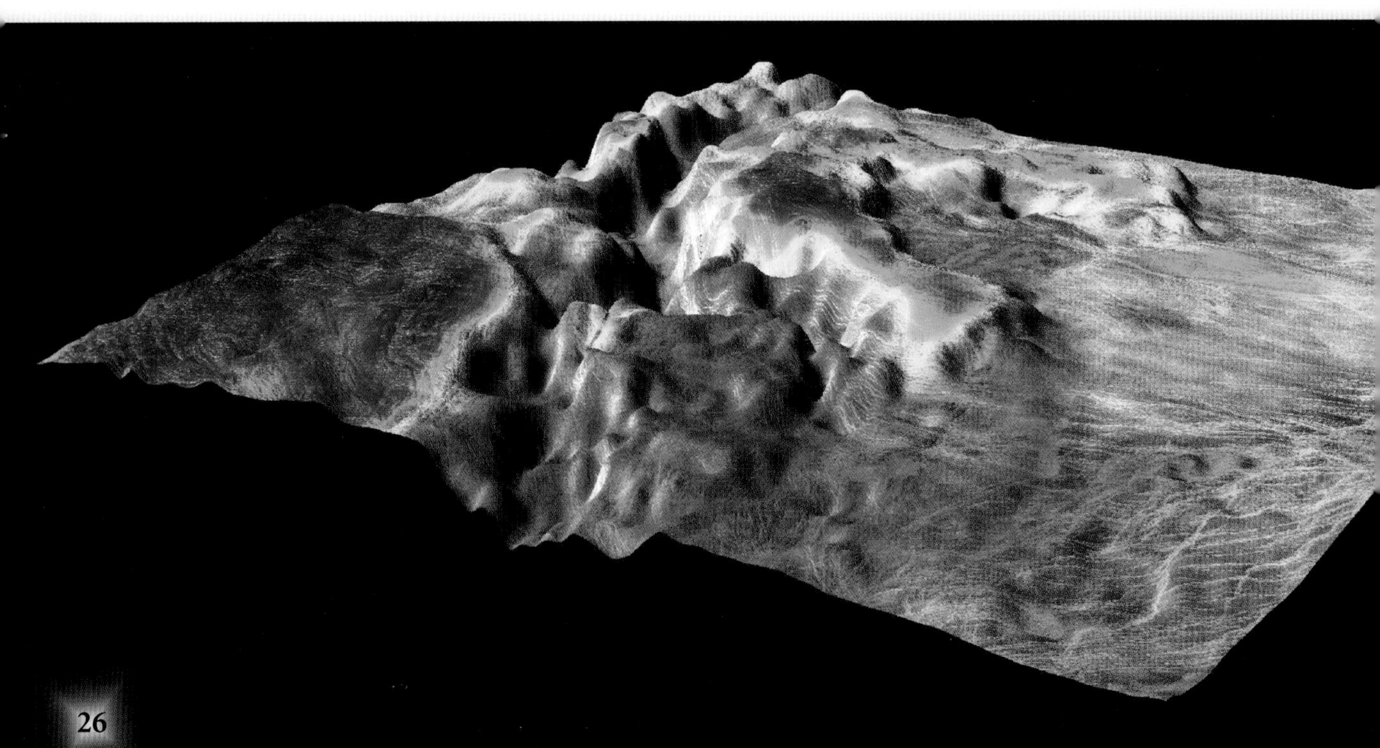

Venus appears to have faulted rocks that splay out like the spokes of a wheel or like rays of sunlight. The land on which they form is broadly domed up, suggesting that hot liquids below once raised the cold, brittle surface rocks and forced them to crack open in a radiating pattern. They are called **NOVAE** and are associated with ring patterns of **FAULTS** called **CORONAE**. Such sites are places of natural weakness in the **CRUST** and so are often places where **VOLCANOES** have also formed.

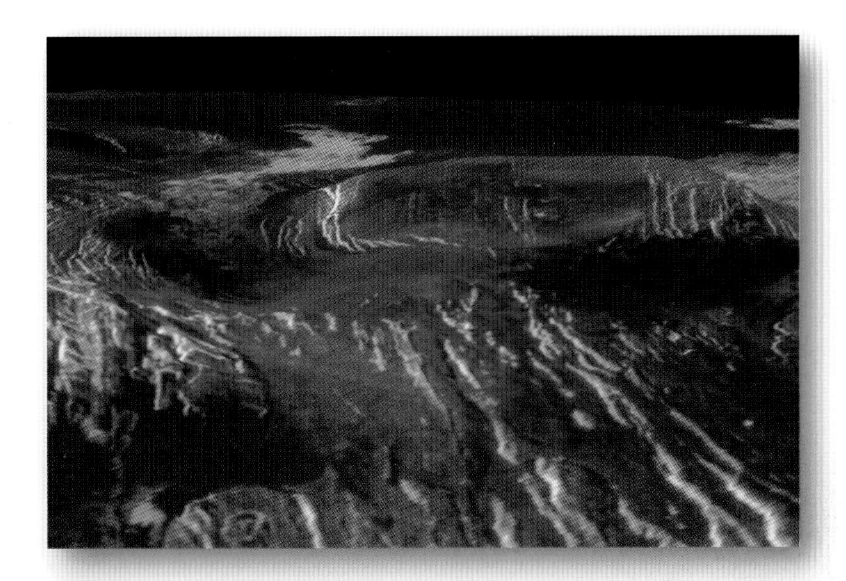

BASIN A large depression in the ground (bigger than a crater).

CHASM A deep, narrow trench.

CORONA (pl. **CORONAE**) A circular to oval pattern of faults, fractures, and ridges with a sagging center as found on Venus.

CRUST The solid outer surface of a rocky body.

FAULT A place in the crust where rocks have fractured, and then one side has moved relative to the other.

FRACTURE A break in brittle rock.

LAVA FLOW A river or sheet of liquid volcanic rock.

MAGMA Hot, melted rock inside the Earth that, when cooled, forms igneous rock.

MOUNTAIN RANGE A long, narrow region of very high land that contains several or many mountains.

NOVA (pl. **NOVAE**) A radiating pattern of faults and fractures unique to Venus.

PLATE A very large unbroken part of the crust of a planet. Also called tectonic plate.

PLATEAU An upland plain or tableland.

RIFT VALLEY A long trench in the surface of a planet produced by the collapse of the crust in a narrow zone.

SCARP The steep slope of a sharp-crested ridge.

VALLEY A natural long depression in the landscape.

VOLCANO A mound or mountain that is formed from ash or lava.

◀ A corona is shown in this computer view of the surface of Venus. The corona has a diameter of 97 kilometers. Lava flows extend for hundreds of kilometers across the fractured plains shown in the background.

Volcanoes

In the early years of the planet there was much volcanic activity. Lava is thought to cover the huge rolling plains and possibly also to have made low hills. Sheets like this can only be formed from runny, basalt lava, and for this reason it is believed that much of the crust is, indeed, basalt.

The biggest volcanoes have produced their own mountains. One of these spectacular mountains is Sif Mons, a **SHIELD VOLCANO** similar to Mauna Loa on Hawaii.

▲ Gula Mons, a kilometer-high volcano, can be seen top left. The impact crater Cunitz, named for the astronomer and mathematician Maria Cunitz, is visible in the center.

▼ Lava flows extend for hundreds of kilometers across the fractured plains at the base of Sif Mons, a volcano with a diameter of 300 kilometers and a height of 2 kilometers.

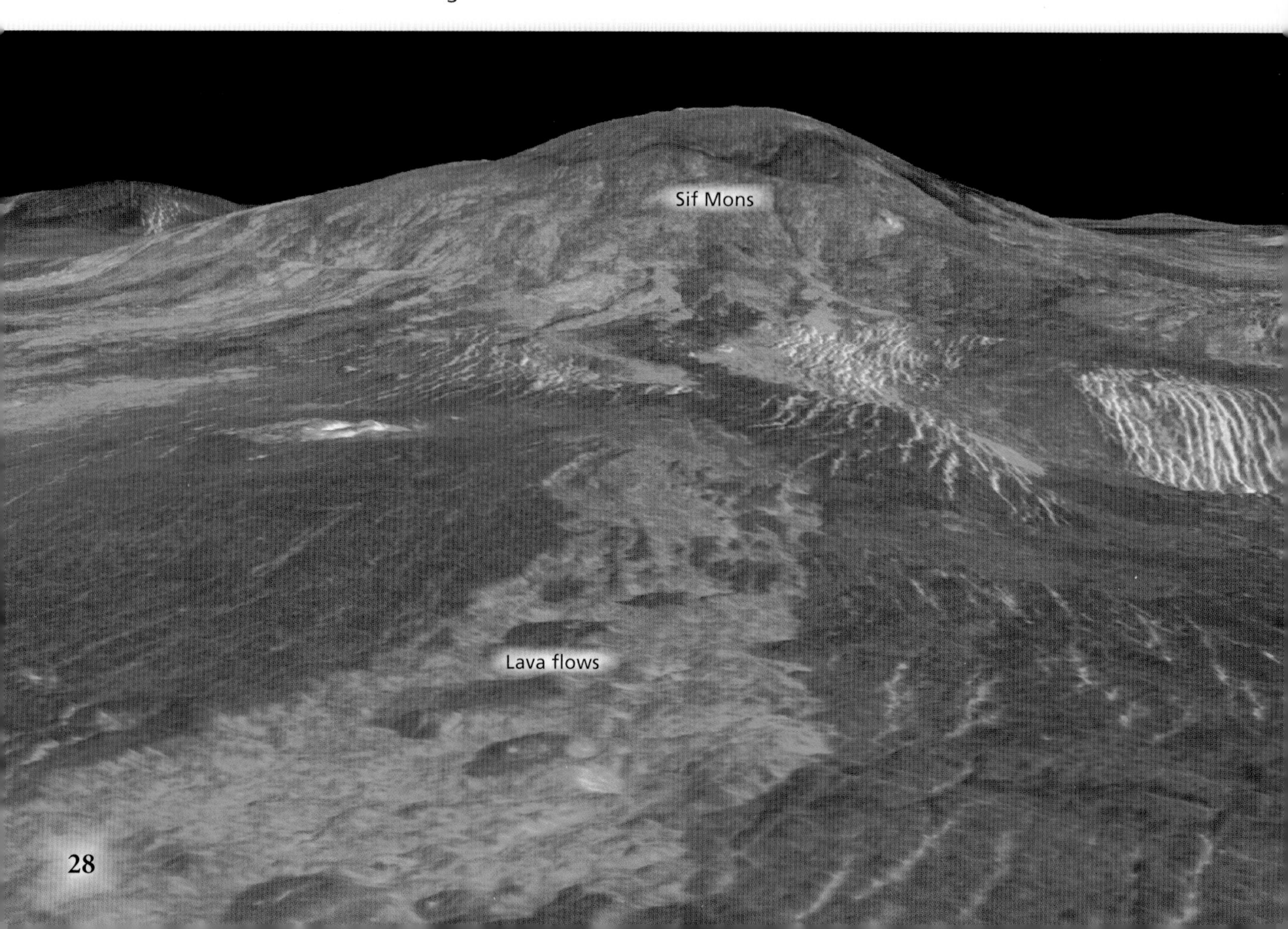

In some cases the upper parts of such volcanoes have collapsed inward under their own weight during a particularly violent episode of eruption. The result is a collapsed cone, or caldera, consisting of a central pit and a tall rim. Sif Mons has such a caldera about 50 kilometers across.

Venus does not just have basaltic volcanoes, however, but also those that have steeper sides. They were probably formed from a more acid kind of lava. They are called pancake domes.

Craters

Although **CRATERS** are less common on the surface than on most other planets, there is still evidence of **METEORITE** impact. Part of the reason for the sparsity of craters may be the dense **ATMOSPHERE** of the planet, which would cause incoming meteorites to burn up, especially small ones that would otherwise have made craters a few kilometers across.

The fact that there are so few craters on the surface of Venus is also a hint that the surface was formed (geologically) relatively recently, and that lava was still flowing less than a billion years ago.

Interior Venus

Venus has a molten **CORE** of metal, a thick **MANTLE** of dense rock, and a surface **CRUST** of cold rock.

The mantle and core are probably very hot as a result of **RADIOACTIVE DECAY** of **ELEMENTS** within the core. So it is likely that some kind of **CONVECTION CURRENTS** work below the crust as they do on the Earth. However, there are major differences between how Venus works and how the Earth works inside. In the case of Venus it seems that where the convection currents well up, they directly produce mountains, and that where convection currents go down, they directly form **DEPRESSIONS**.

What this suggests is that although Venus is still a very active geological planet, it does not have crustal **PLATES** moving over its surface, as does the Earth.

ATMOSPHERE The envelope of gases that surrounds the Earth and other bodies in the universe.

CONVECTION CURRENTS The circulating flow in a fluid (liquid or gas) that occurs when it is heated from below.

CORE The central region of a body.

CRATER A deep bowl-shaped depression in the surface of a body formed by the high-speed impact of another, smaller body.

CRUST The solid outer surface of a rocky body.

DEPRESSION A sunken area or hollow in a surface or landscape.

ELEMENT A substance that cannot be decomposed into simpler substances by chemical means.

MANTLE The region of a planet between the core and the crust.

METEORITE A meteor that reaches the Earth's surface.

PLATE A very large unbroken part of the crust of a planet. Also called tectonic plate.

RADIOACTIVE DECAY The change that takes place inside radioactive materials and causes them to give out progressively less radiation over time.

SHIELD VOLCANO A volcanic cone that is broad and gently sloping.

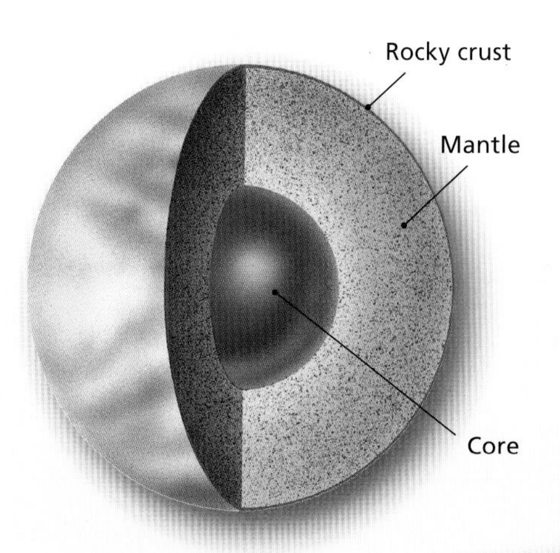

4: MARS

Mars, known as the red planet because of its apparent color when seen from the Earth, is the fourth planet from the Sun and our nearest neighbor moving away from the Sun.

It is quite a small planet, being seventh out of nine in the order of planet sizes, only half the diameter of the Earth and a tenth of its **MASS**. As a result, its **GRAVITY** is just a third of that experienced on Earth.

▲ The Mars Global Surveyor was launched in November 1996 to study the surface features, atmosphere, and magnetic properties of Mars.

▼ Mars taken by NASA's **HUBBLE SPACE TELESCOPE** when Mars was 87 million kilometers from Earth. From this distance the telescope could see Martian features as small as 19 kilometers wide.

The four hemispheric views have been combined into a full-color global map.

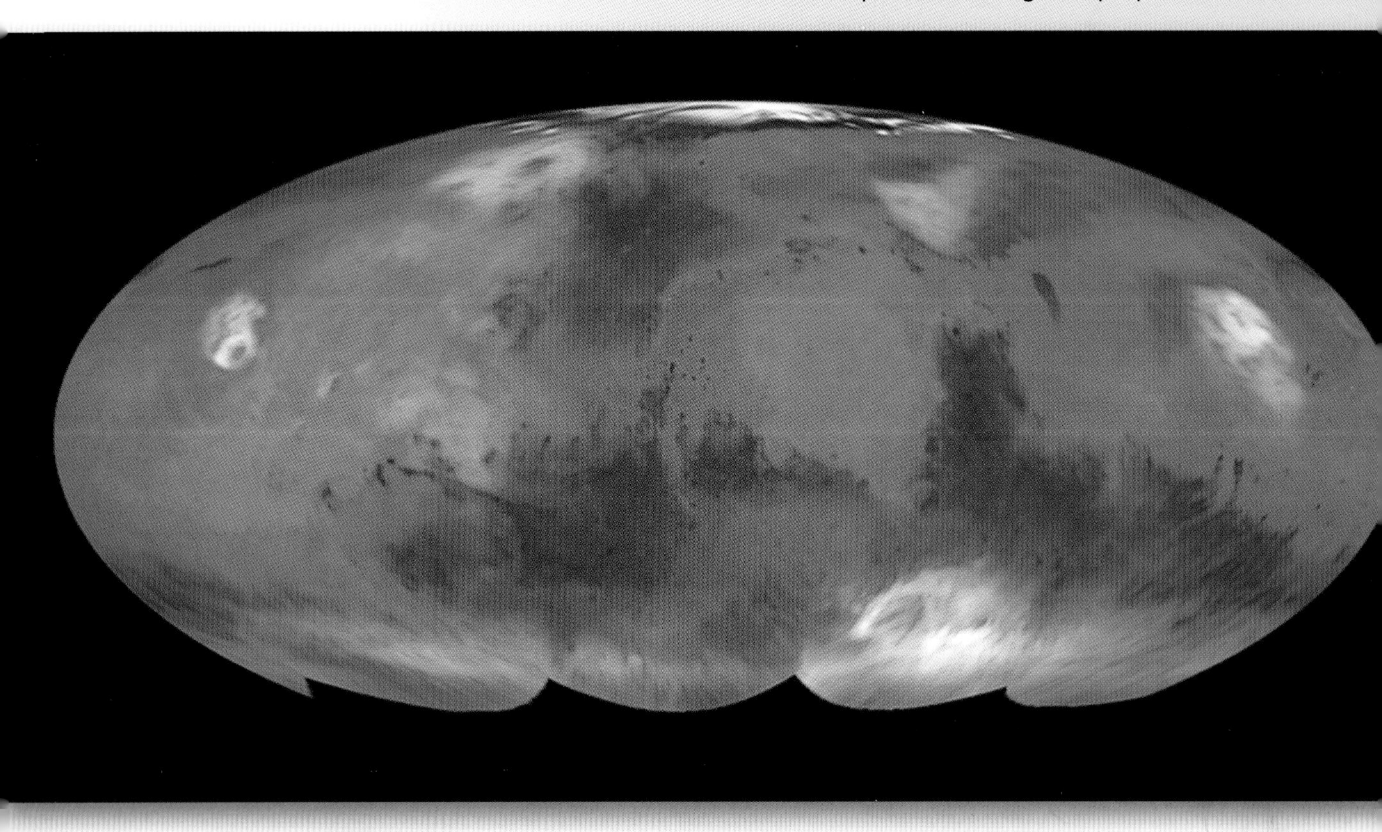

For more on the Hubble Space Telescope see Volume 8: *What satellites see*.

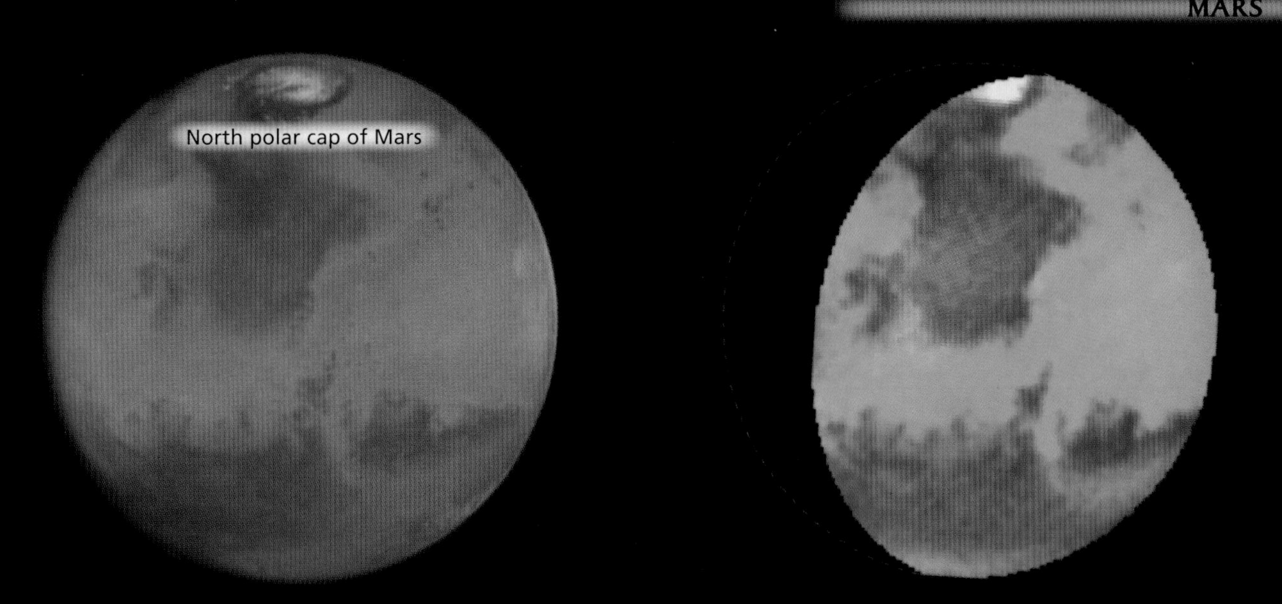

▲ This "true-color" image *(top left)* of Mars shows the planet as it looks to human eyes. The slightly bluer shade along the edges of the disk is due to atmospheric hazes and wispy water-ice clouds. The yellowish-pink color of the northern polar **ICE CAP** indicates the presence of small iron-bearing dust particles in the air above the blue-white water-ice and carbon-dioxide-ice of the polar cap. Hubble's **FALSE-COLOR** picture *(top right)* reveals water-bearing **MINERALS** on the planet. Reddish regions show where they are most common. In particular, the large reddish region known as Mare Acidalium was the site of massive flooding early in Martian history.

Martian orbit and rotation

Mars orbits the Sun once in 687 Earth days at a distance of about one and a half times as far from the Sun as the Earth is.

A Martian year is about twice as long as an Earth year. The days are, however, remarkably similar, the Martian day being 24 hours and 37 minutes.

Mars orbits the Sun in a very pronounced oval, or ellipse. That means it comes closer to both the Sun and the Earth as it completes each **ORBIT**. At its nearest Mars is 207 million kilometers from the Sun and 56 million kilometers from the Earth, but it can be as much as 250 million kilometers from the Sun and 400 million kilometers from the Earth. As a result, we see Mars change size from month to month.

As Mars gets closer to the Sun, it **REFLECTS** more light and so appears brighter in the sky. That is why Mars is sometimes very clear and bright, and at other times it is dim. The **PLANE** in which Mars orbits is not the same as that of the Earth, and it is closest to the Earth when it can be seen from the southern hemisphere.

FALSE COLOR The colors used to make the appearance of some property more obvious.

GRAVITY The force of attraction between bodies.

HUBBLE SPACE TELESCOPE An orbiting telescope (and so a satellite) that was placed above the Earth's atmosphere so that it could take images that were far clearer than anything that could be obtained from the surface of the Earth.

ICE CAP A small mountainous region that is covered in ice.

MASS The amount of matter in an object.

MINERAL A solid crystalline substance.

ORBIT The path followed by one object as it tracks around another.

PLANE A flat surface.

REFLECT To bounce back any light that falls on a surface.

Mars spins on an **AXIS** that tilts at about 25° from the plane of its orbit (the Earth's axis tilts at 23.5°). As a result, Mars has seasons during its orbit. But because the orbit of the planet is an oval, the seasons are very uneven in length (while the Earth's seasons are roughly the same). This means that the northern summer is longer than on Earth. Because Mars is also far from the Sun at this time, the summers are cool. The southern summers are correspondingly shorter; but since the planet is then close to the Sun, the southern summer is warm.

Ice caps

ICE CAPS are a very striking feature of Mars. Unlike the Earth, where ice caps are more or less the same size from one century to another and many hundreds and even thousands of meters thick, Martian ice caps are very thin, a matter of a few meters or tens of meters. This lack of ice thickness explains why they can change size so rapidly, why Martian ice caps can shrink by as much as a degree of **LATITUDE** every 5 days, and why by summer they have almost vanished. Similarly, as winter approaches, they grow quickly almost half way to the **EQUATOR**.

Polar ice caps

▶ These images are from NASA's Hubble Space Telescope.

(Top) Early spring in the northern hemisphere: The cap extends down to 60°N latitude, nearly its maximum winter extent. (The notches are areas where Hubble data was not available.) The cap is actually fairly circular around the geographic **POLE** at this season; the bluish "knobs" where the cap seems to extend further are clouds.

(Middle) Midspring, and warmth has caused the carbon dioxide ice and frost to change back into vapor.

(Bottom) Early summer, and the cap has fully retreated to its remnant core of water-ice. This leftover cap is actually almost cut into two by a large, horn-shaped canyon called Chasma Borealis, which slices deeply into the polar terrain.

▼ The icy surface of Mars.

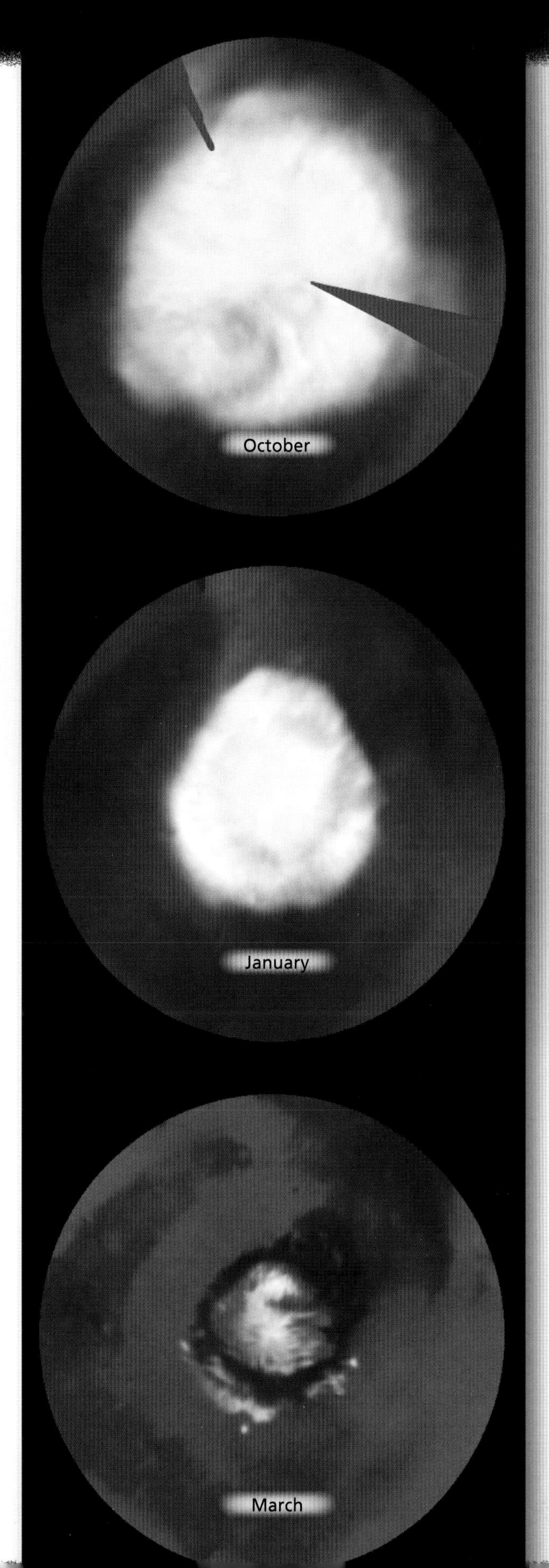

AXIS (pl. **AXES**) The line around which a body spins.

EQUATOR The ring drawn around a body midway between the poles.

GRAVITY The force of attraction between bodies.

ICE CAP A small mountainous region that is covered in ice.

LATITUDE Angular distance north or south of the equator, measured through 90°.

POLE The geographic pole is the place where a line drawn along the axis of rotation exits from a body's surface.

The ice cap is made primarily of solid carbon dioxide, which is dry ice. As the ice cap grows, cloud made of water-ice and dry ice forms over and beyond it, reaching well beyond the extent of the ice cap. That makes it difficult to see part of the planet from the Earth.

The northern ice cap lasts longer than the southern one due to the colder summer. By summer what is left of the ice cap is not dry ice but water, which is much harder to melt than dry ice and will only melt at much higher temperatures. So it seems that there is a polar core of frozen water that is covered and extended by dry ice each winter.

Atmosphere

Mars is notorious for its dust storms. They can be built up by the winds to completely cover the surface. Because the **GRAVITY** on Mars is only a third of that on the Earth, it is easier for the winds to pick up dust and keep it suspended.

A blue haze that sometimes occurs is probably caused by the dust in the air (see top picture on page 31).

▼ These are pictures of storm clouds brewing over the north polar cap of Mars. These images show that Mars has weather systems as complex and exciting as the Earth's.

The four still-frame images follow the evolution of a storm system that developed over the Martian north pole. The pictures were taken at approximately 2-hour intervals. The north polar ice cap is the white feature at the center of each frame. Clouds that appear white consist mainly of water-ice. Clouds that appear orange-brown contain dust.

Mars has a very thin **ATMOSPHERE** compared to that of the Earth, and most of it (94% by weight) is carbon dioxide. **PRESSURE** on the surface is about 1% of that on the Earth. There is only a small amount of free oxygen, together with some nitrogen, **NOBLE GASES**, and traces of **WATER VAPOR**. Most of them were lost long ago from the air to space.

In winter a large proportion of the carbon dioxide turns to dry ice and falls like snow on the ice caps. This dry ice then **EVAPORATES** again in summer.

The average daytime surface temperature of the planet is about –23°C, with the air even colder at –73°C.

The air contains white clouds made from water that has frozen to ice crystals and yellow clouds made entirely of dust.

Temperature contrasts

The amount of water vapor in the air is tiny, but it is likely that some kind of cycling occurs between the water vapor in the air and the water found as ice in the soil.

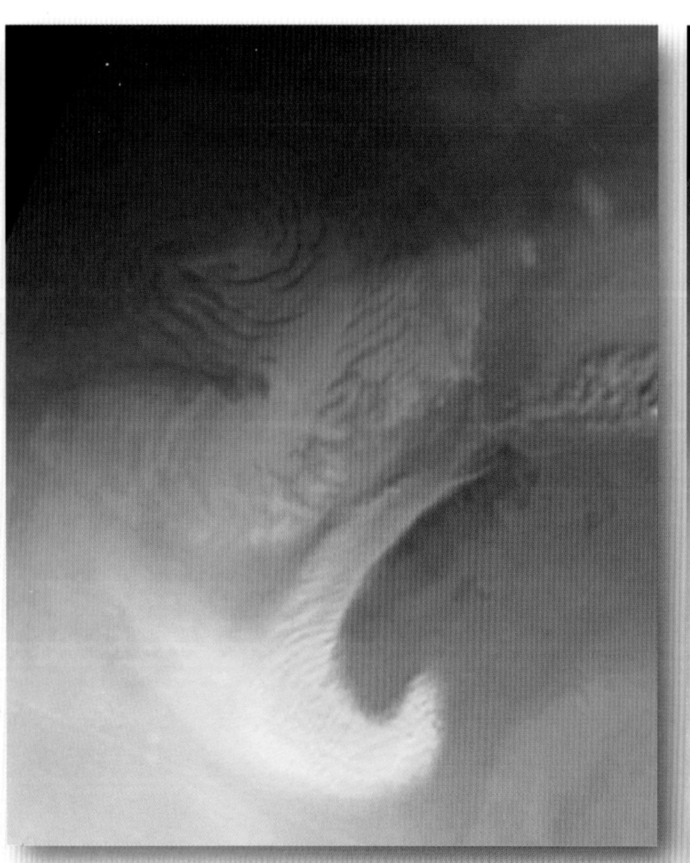

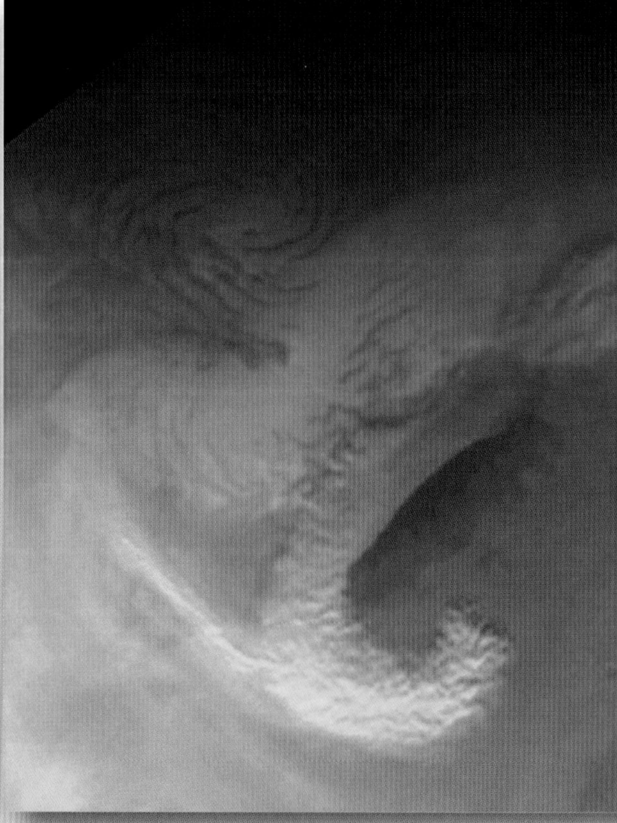

ATMOSPHERE The envelope of gases that surrounds the Earth and other bodies in the universe.

EVAPORATE The change in state from liquid to a gas.

NOBLE GASES The unreactive gases, such as neon, xenon, and krypton.

PRESSURE The force per unit area.

WATER VAPOR The gaseous form of water. Also sometimes referred to as moisture.

◀ Frosty white water-ice clouds and swirling orange dust storms above a vivid rusty landscape reveal Mars as a dynamic planet.

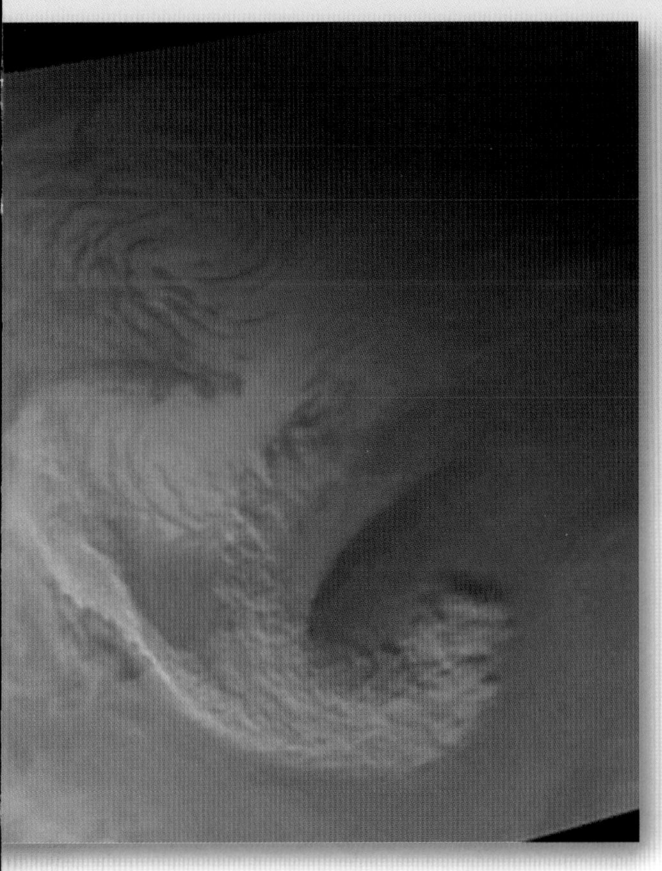

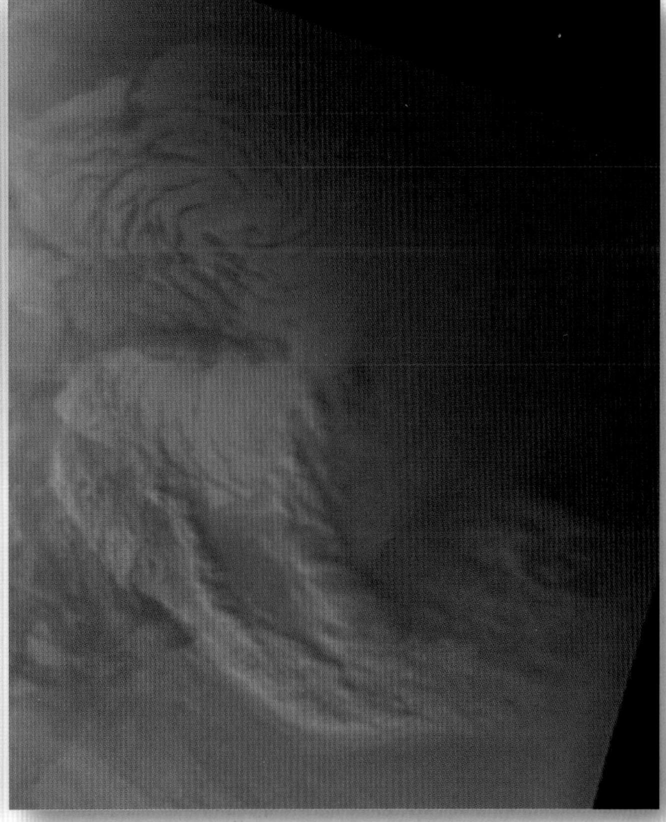

On Earth carbon dioxide is a very important GREENHOUSE EFFECT gas—it strongly absorbs heat radiated from the surface of the planet. However, at the much lower temperatures of Mars it radiates heat very efficiently, and any heat absorbed in the air is not therefore due to carbon dioxide but to dust suspended in the air.

Without a blanket of cloud or WATER VAPOR in the air there is little to trap the heat either from the Sun or from the surface of Mars. So each day the temperature fluctuates wildly in the air close to the ground, heating up during the daytime and falling again at night. The temperature changes from –84°C just before sunrise to –33°C in early afternoon, far greater than anything on Earth. When there are dust storms, the dust absorbs heat, and so changes are somewhat smaller.

On Earth there are huge oceans. The water absorbs heat and also helps steady the temperatures and give coastal regions a more stable temperature range than inland areas. On Mars, with no oceans, such an effect is absent.

Ice, wind, and sand

What does have an effect is the size of the ICE CAPS that change in area dramatically throughout each year (growing at the pole experiencing winter, and shrinking at the pole experiencing summer—see pages 32–33). That means regions of intense ice-cap cold can be close to regions that are heated by sunshine. In turn, that causes air to flow by the process of CONVECTION. As this air moves, it is deflected from a direct path between the warmer and colder regions by the spin of the planet, which causes a complicated wind pattern.

In some places winds can become very strong, accounting for the buildup of the dust storms. With such a lot of dust in the air the heating of the air changes again, and the winds die down, allowing the dust to settle. That explains why dust storms tend to be a more or less regular feature.

SAND DUNES surround the northern ice cap. They are most likely a result of the strongest winds blowing close to the point where land and ice cap meet.

Dust storm

▶ A global dust storm engulfs Mars with the onset of Martian spring in the southern hemisphere. Such storms rage for months on end, obscuring all surface features. The fine airborne dust blocks a significant amount of sunlight from reaching the Martian surface.

Viking on Mars

▶ This boulder-strewn field of red rocks reaches to the horizon nearly 3 kilometers from Viking 2 on Mars' Utopian Plain.

The Viking mission was composed of two spacecraft—Viking 1 and Viking 2—each consisting of an orbiter and a lander. They both landed on Mars in 1976.

CONVECTION The circulating flow in a fluid (liquid or gas) that occurs when it is heated from below.

GREENHOUSE EFFECT The increase in atmospheric temperature produced by the presence of carbon dioxide in the air.

ICE CAP A small mountainous region that is covered in ice.

SAND DUNE An aerodynamically shaped hump of sand.

WATER VAPOR The gaseous form of water. Also sometimes referred to as moisture.

The surface

Mars has been the subject of much speculation over the centuries. For a long time the bright areas were thought to be seas and so were named *maria* (Latin for "oceans"). However, it is now known that the surface is essentially a desert.

Running across the surface are dark areas made up of alignments of **CRATERS**, **RIDGES**, and hills.

The lines running across the bright **MARIA** were often referred to in the past as canals but are now thought to be produced by the way dust is moved around by the Martian winds.

It was also discovered that the surface of Mars is quite varied, with some featureless areas, some highlands, some enormous **VOLCANOES**, and some areas that seemed to have been formed chaotically.

▲ A piece of Mars that landed in Antarctica as a **METEORITE**. It gave vital clues to the nature of the red planet.

▼ This spectacular picture of the Martian landscape by the Viking 1 lander shows a dune field with features remarkably similar to many seen in the deserts of Earth. The large boulder in the center is about 8 meters from the spacecraft and measures about 1 x 3 meters.

The Valles Marineris

▼ This picture of Mars shows the entire Valles Marineris canyon system, over 3,000 km long and up to 8 km deep.

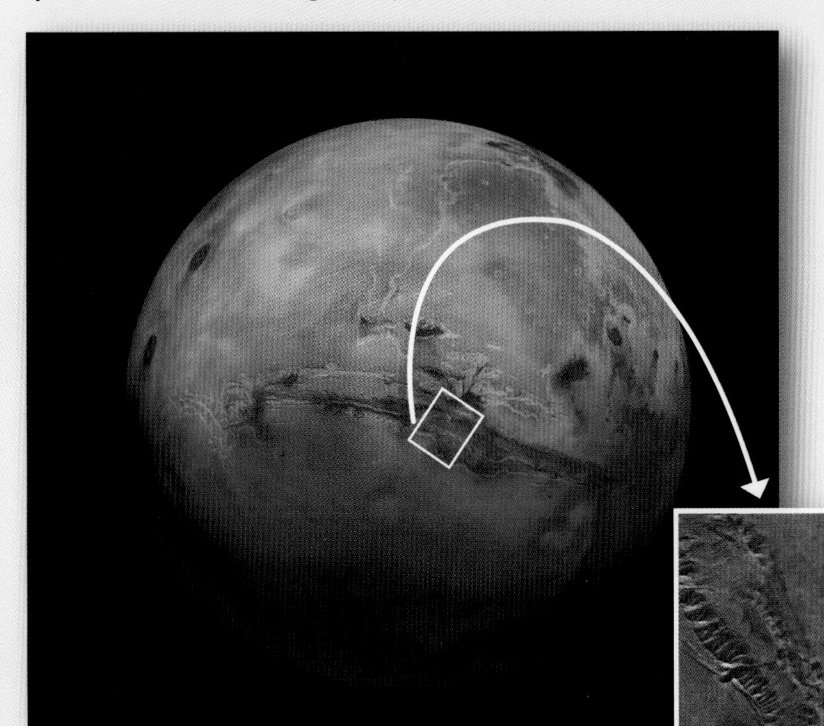

▶ This picture shows the Melas **CHASM** and a portion of Candor Chasm *(upper right)* in central Valles Marineris.

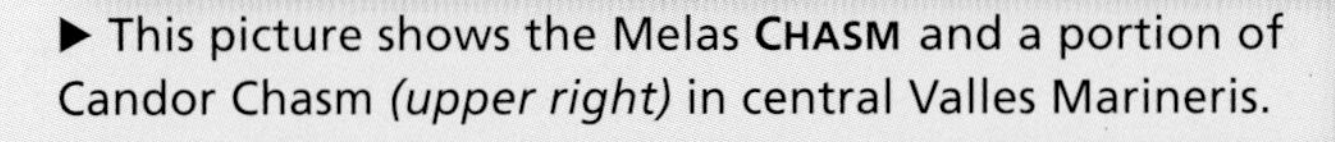

CHASM A deep, narrow trench.

CRATER A deep bowl-shaped depression in the surface of a body formed by the high-speed impact of another, smaller body.

MARE (pl. **MARIA**) A flat, dark plain created by lava flows.

METEORITE A meteor that reaches the Earth's surface.

RIDGE A narrow crest of an upland area.

VOLCANO A mound or mountain that is formed from ash or lava.

There is an enormous range of heights on Mars. Olympus Mons, whose base has a diameter of 550 kilometers, is the biggest volcano on Mars and has a staggering volume ten times the volume of the Earth's largest volcano, while its height is a phenomenal 27 kilometers above average surface level, or three times that of Mount Everest (Mount Everest on Earth is 8,848 km).

Mars is a planet of contrasts so far unexplained. Its southern hemisphere is heavily cratered, while the northern hemisphere has gently undulating (rolling) plains. The cratered area is much higher than the plains.

In the solar system it is generally assumed that heavily cratered surfaces are very old because the number of meteoroids hitting planets is now far smaller than in the early days of the formation of the planets. On the other hand, smooth plains, as on parts of Mars, are normally thought to show a young surface because the smoothness must be due to some action, for example, **LAVA FLOWS** or the spreading of sand and mud under water.

Mars' biggest volcano

▲ Olympus Mons is taller than three Mount Everests and about as wide as the entire Hawaiian Island chain. Its flanks are very gently sloping—typically 2° to 5°.

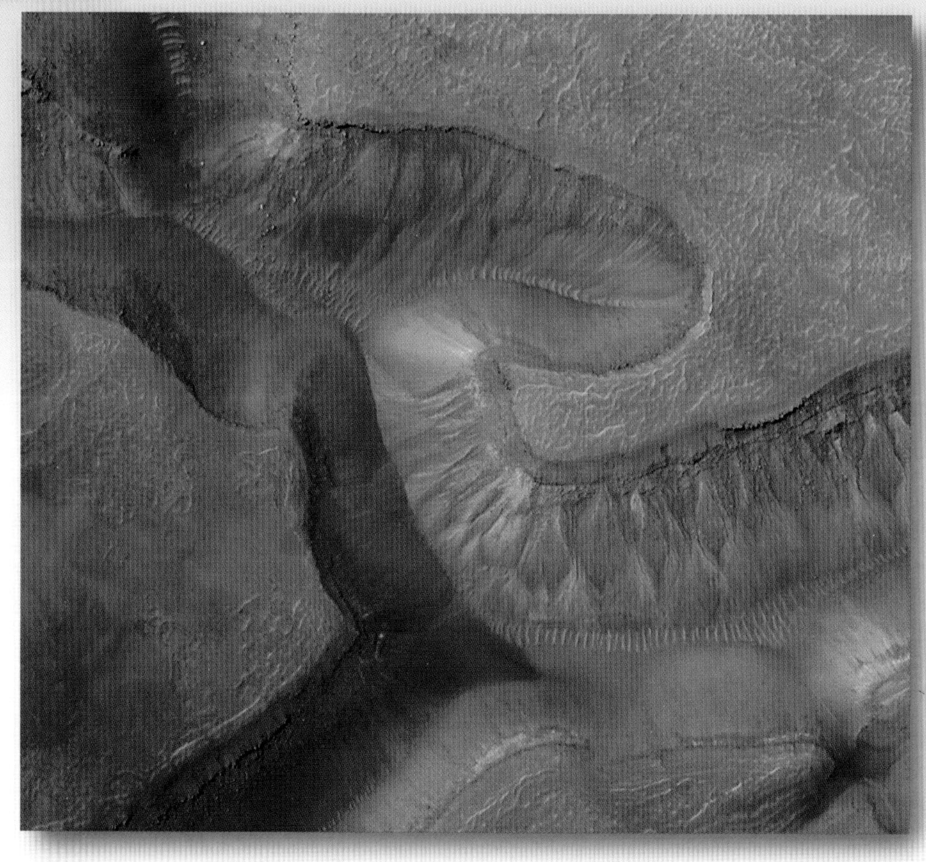

Evidence for recent liquid water on Mars

▶ This picture shows many Martian **GULLIES** believed to have been eroded by water only a few years ago. It is possible that this area has water seeping out of the ground today.

The largest crater is the Hellas Basin, which is about 1,600 kilometers across. The largest volcanoes, on the other hand, are in the northern hemisphere. They are grouped into two areas, called Tharsis and Elysium. Tharsis is a high-level plain that rises 10 kilometers above the average Martian surface. Sticking up from it are the volcanoes Arsia Mons, Pavonis Mons, and Ascraeus Mons. On the edge of the Tharsis plain stands Olympus Mons. The surface of the high-level plain is cracked by wide gashes such as Valles Marineris (see page 39), whose length is about a quarter of the **CIRCUMFERENCE** of the planet. It is 7 to 10 km deep and is something like the East African rift valley on Earth. The sides of the rift have spectacular **LANDSLIDES**. In the sides of these **RIFTS** the rocks are exposed, giving the impression of layers of rock that could only have been formed under water.

Elysium is a much smaller high-level plain, about 6 kilometers above average land level and topped by the volcanoes Hecates Tholus, Elysium Mons, and Albor Tholus.

What are missing are the long mountain ranges we see on Earth. As a result, it is unlikely that the same forces act on the Martian **CRUST** as act on the Earth's crust—there cannot be any moving **PLATES** to collide.

CIRCUMFERENCE The distance around the edge of a circle or sphere.

CRUST The solid outer surface of a rocky body.

FALSE COLOR The colors used to make the appearance of some property more obvious.

GULLY (pl. **GULLIES**) A trench in the land surface formed, on Earth, by running water.

LANDSLIDE A sudden collapse of material on a steep slope.

LAVA FLOW A river or sheet of liquid volcanic rock.

PLATE A very large unbroken part of the crust of a planet. Also called tectonic plate.

RIFT A trench made by the sinking of a part of the crust between parallel faults.

Hellas Basin

◀▲ These maps are global **FALSE-COLOR** views of Mars. The top image shows the Hellas Basin *(bottom left)*. The left-hand image shows the four largest volcanoes in Tharsis, forming a triangle *(center left)*.

◀ Phobos, one of Mars' two satellites.

Moons

Two dark-colored tiny **MOONS** are in **ORBIT** around Mars. They are called Phobos and Deimos. They may have once been **ASTEROIDS** that were captured by Mars during the early stages of its formation. Both rotate on their **AXES** at the same rate as they spin around the planet. This is similar to the Earth's Moon.

Phobos goes around Mars in just over seven and a half hours, so that it rises and sets twice in a Martian day. It is a potato-shaped and heavily cratered moon, with its longest axis pointing toward the planet.

Phobos orbits at just under two Mars **RADII** from the surface of the planet. It is so close to Mars that it cannot be seen from everywhere on the planet in the way that we can see the Earth's Moon. Instead, it can only be seen from fairly close to the equator.

Because it is so close to the surface, it is strongly influenced by the **GRAVITY** on Mars, which is continually slowing it down. In the future it is likely that it will collide with the surface of the planet.

Interestingly, smaller Deimos, which has a smooth surface, is so far away that the Martian gravity actually pushes the moon away from the planet. Like Phobos, it is a potato-shaped moon, with its longest axis pointing toward the planet. Deimos appears to be covered with fine dust.

up gases that gradually formed the Martian atmosphere. None of the volcanoes appears active today, so the heat that produced the molten rock must have all been lost to space some time ago.

The surface of the crust has been broken down into a clay soil, but that must have happened a long time ago.

large natural satellite of a planet.

ORBIT The path followed by one object as it tracks around another.

RADIOACTIVE The property of some materials that emit radiation or energetic particles from the nucleus of their atoms.

RADIUS (pl. **RADII**) The distance from the center to the outside of a circle or sphere.

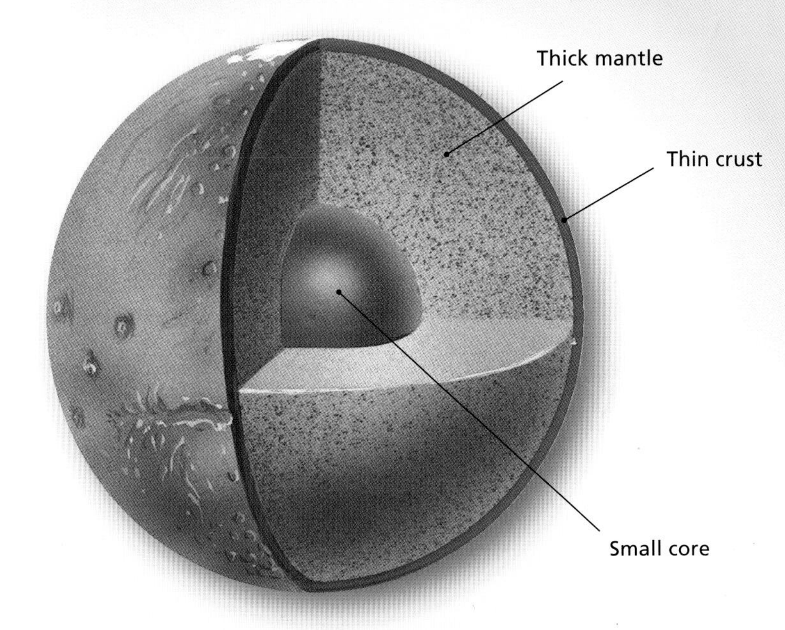

◀ The structure of Mars. A thin crust surrounds a thick mantle, which, in turn, encloses a small core.

▲ This is the clearest view yet of the distant planet Pluto and its moon, Charon, as revealed by NASA's **HUBBLE SPACE TELESCOPE**. Pluto is nearly 30 times as far from the Sun as the Earth is.

Hubble's picture allows the diameters of Pluto (2,320 kilometers) and Charon (1,270 kilometers) to be measured accurately for the first time.

Charon is bluer than Pluto. That means both worlds have different surface compositions and structures.

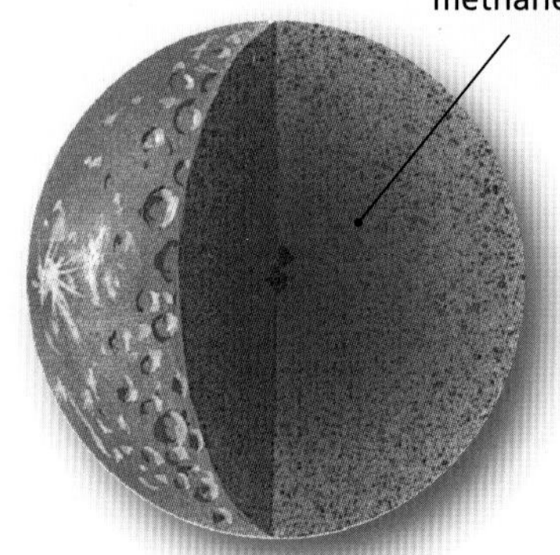

5: PLUTO

Pluto is normally thought of as the known planet furthest from the Sun because its average distance from the Sun is 5.9 billion km. But the **ORBIT** of Pluto is a squashed oval (called an eccentric orbit). So from time to time Pluto is actually closer to the Sun than **NEPTUNE** is.

Very little is known about Pluto. It was not discovered until 1930, and that was only because scientists at that time thought that the orbits of Uranus and Neptune were being affected by another unseen planet somewhere on the edge of the solar system. In fact, scientists were wrong, and the orbits are not affected by Pluto; but by accident this idea made them look in just the place where Pluto lies. To these first observers it looked like a dim star; but as they compared pictures taken over time, they saw that it moved against the background of stars, and so it had to be a distant planet.

Far away, small, and dim

Pluto is so far away that it appears as a faint blur even through high-powered telescopes. From Pluto the Sun would appear only as a bright star. It takes 5 hours for sunlight to reach the planet. However, within a six-day period it changes in its apparent brightness by 12%, suggesting that it is not a planet with a uniform surface. From this observation it is believed the rotation of Pluto on its **AXIS** happens about once every 6 days.

Pluto spins on its axis nearly on its side. It also spins in the opposite direction from the Earth (called a retrograde direction), so that the Sun rises in the west and sets in the east (as it does on Venus).

Pluto is about 2,300 km across (about half the size of Mercury or two-thirds the size of the Earth's Moon). It has a low **DENSITY** for a rocky planet, on the order of 2 g/cm^3. That is less than half of the density of the Earth and only twice that of some of the gas giant planets. For this reason it cannot be solid rock. Rather, it may well be a mixture of rock and solid methane (gas).

The surface of Pluto is most likely reddish, with the methane in the surface making the planet quite **REFLECTIVE** (three times as reflective as our Moon).

AXIS (pl. **AXES**) The line around which a body spins.

BASIN A large depression in the ground (bigger than a crater).

CRATER A deep bowl-shaped depression in the surface of a body formed by the high-speed impact of another, smaller body.

DENSITY A measure of the amount of matter in a space.

HUBBLE SPACE TELESCOPE An orbiting telescope (and so a satellite) that was placed above the Earth's atmosphere so that it could take images that were far clearer than anything that could be obtained from the surface of the Earth.

NEPTUNE The eighth planet from the Sun in our solar system and five planets farther away from the Sun than the Earth.

ORBIT The path followed by one object as it tracks around another.

REFLECTIVE To bounce back any light that falls on a surface.

▼ This is the first image of the surface map of Pluto taken from NASA's Hubble Space Telescope. Hubble imaged nearly the entire surface as Pluto rotated on its axis.

Pluto has a dark equatorial belt and bright polar caps. The variations in brightness may be due to features such as **BASINS** and **CRATERS**.

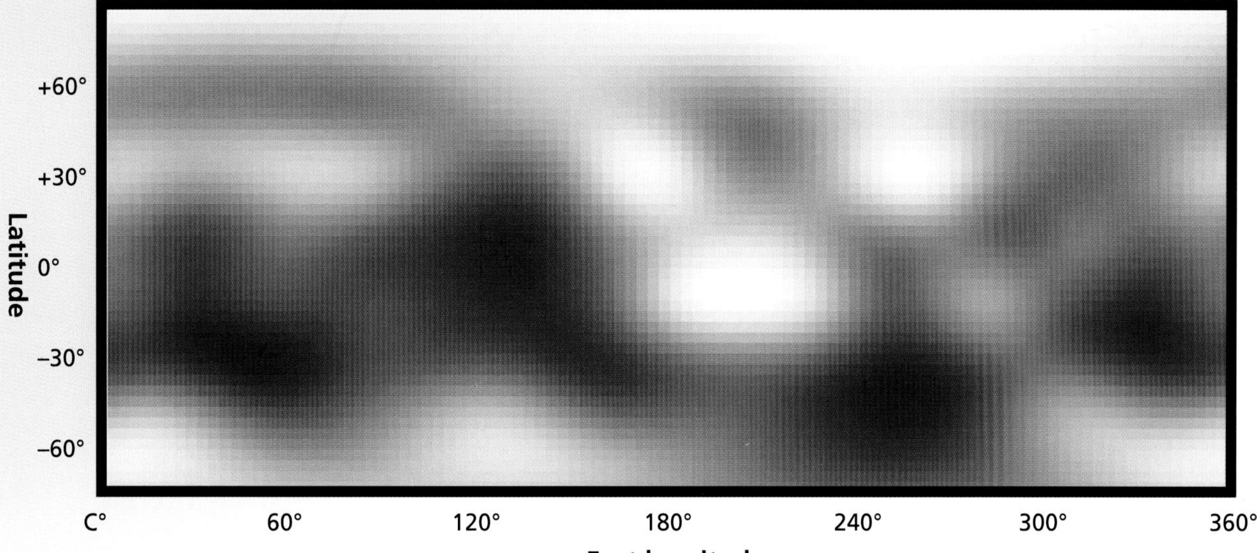

It probably has an extremely thin **ATMOSPHERE** of methane gas, with a **PRESSURE** about a millionth of that on Earth.

Pluto is a cold world, getting just a sixteen-hundredths of the heating that the Earth's surface gets. As a result, it has an average temperature of just about 50° above **ABSOLUTE ZERO** (approximately –220°C). Again, because it has such an oddly shaped orbit, Pluto is sometimes much farther away from the Sun than at other times, so its surface temperature varies considerably around this average value.

Pluto has a "moon" about half the size of the planet, called Charon. It was not discovered until 1978. Before then it was thought to be a bump on the surface of Pluto. The orbit of Charon keeps time exactly with the spin of Pluto (a so-called **SYNCHRONOUS ORBIT**). This unique relationship means that Charon can only ever be seen from one side of Pluto. Furthermore, like most moons, it is in **SYNCHRONOUS ROTATION**, and so it always keeps the same side of itself to the planet.

Charon is more gray than Pluto, and it contains water-ice rather than solid methane (called methane-ice).

Because Charon is relatively similar in size to Pluto, many astronomers call the Pluto-Charon system a "double planet."

▼ An artist's impression of the surface of Pluto looking toward Charon.

▶ An artist's impression of the **MINOR PLANET** Quaoar.

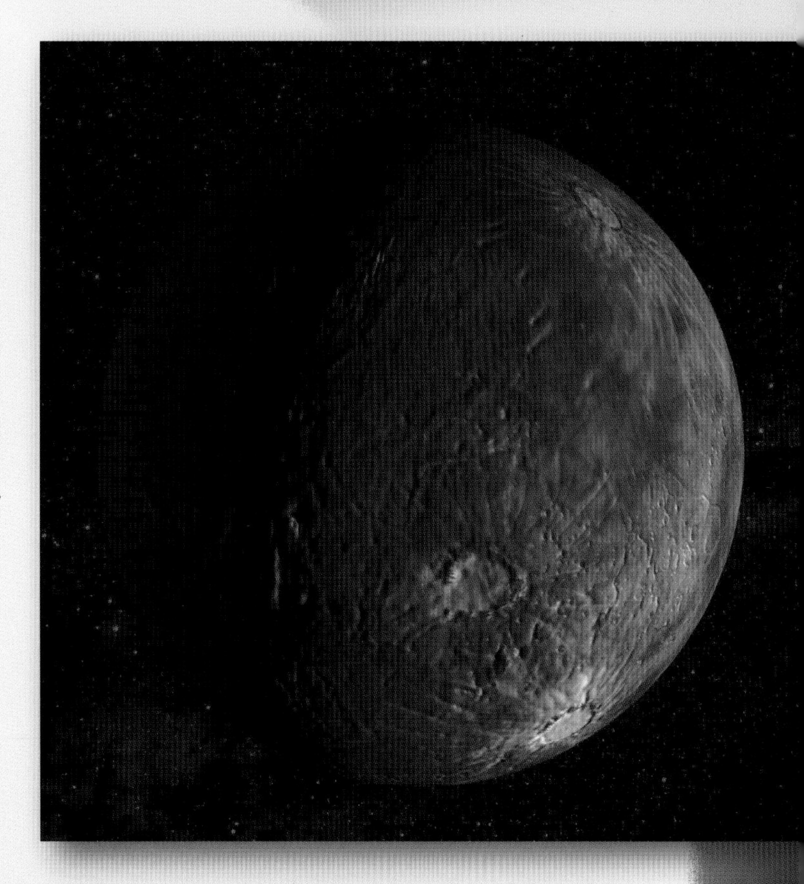

Pluto resembles Triton, one of Neptune's moons. But since Charon and Pluto are different in composition, it is likely that Charon is the result of a collision between Pluto and some unknown body, which resulted in debris that then grouped together as the moon. However, with so little measurement available, nobody is sure about the origin of either Pluto or Charon.

Pluto and the Kuiper belt

Pluto lies in a region distant from the Sun that contains many other rocky bodies. Only recently discovered, it is called the **KUIPER BELT**. It is an icy debris field of cometlike bodies extending 11 billion kilometers beyond Neptune's orbit. Over the past decade more than 500 icy worlds have been found in the Kuiper belt. With a few exceptions all have been significantly smaller than Pluto.

Quaoar, for example, is about seven billion kilometers away from Earth, well over 1.6 billion kilometers farther away than Pluto. Unlike Pluto, its orbit around the Sun is very circular, even more so than most of the planetary-class bodies in the solar system. It is the farthest object in the solar system ever to be detected by a telescope.

ABSOLUTE ZERO The coldest possible temperature, defined as 0 K or –273°C.

ATMOSPHERE The envelope of gases that surrounds the Earth and other bodies in the universe.

KUIPER BELT A belt of planetesimals (small rocky bodies, one kilometer to hundreds of kilometers across) much closer to the Sun than the Oort cloud (see page 55).

MINOR PLANET Another term for an asteroid.

PRESSURE The force per unit area.

SYNCHRONOUS ORBIT An orbit in which a satellite (such as a moon) moves around a planet in the same time that it takes for the planet to make one rotation on its axis.

SYNCHRONOUS ROTATION When two bodies make a complete rotation on their axes in the same time.

6: SMALL ROCKY BODIES

Asteroids

ASTEROIDS are rocky bodies that **ORBIT** the Sun mainly in the **ASTEROID BELT** between Mars and Jupiter.

Asteroids are also known as minor planets, but no asteroid is more than about 1,000 kilometers in diameter.

About 5% lie outside the main asteroid belt or have very oddly shaped orbits. One even comes closer to the Sun than Mercury on part of its orbit. These bodies may be former **COMETS**, but at present they are still classed as asteroids.

The first asteroid was seen from the Earth in 1801. It was called Ceres. After this, four more faint objects were observed. They are now known as Pallas, Juno, Vesta, and Astraea. All of the others are smaller and fainter, and so were only discovered after much searching.

▲ An asteroid is shown here as the long blue streak.

▼ The asteroid belt lies between Mars and Jupiter. The two planets are shown here for reference.

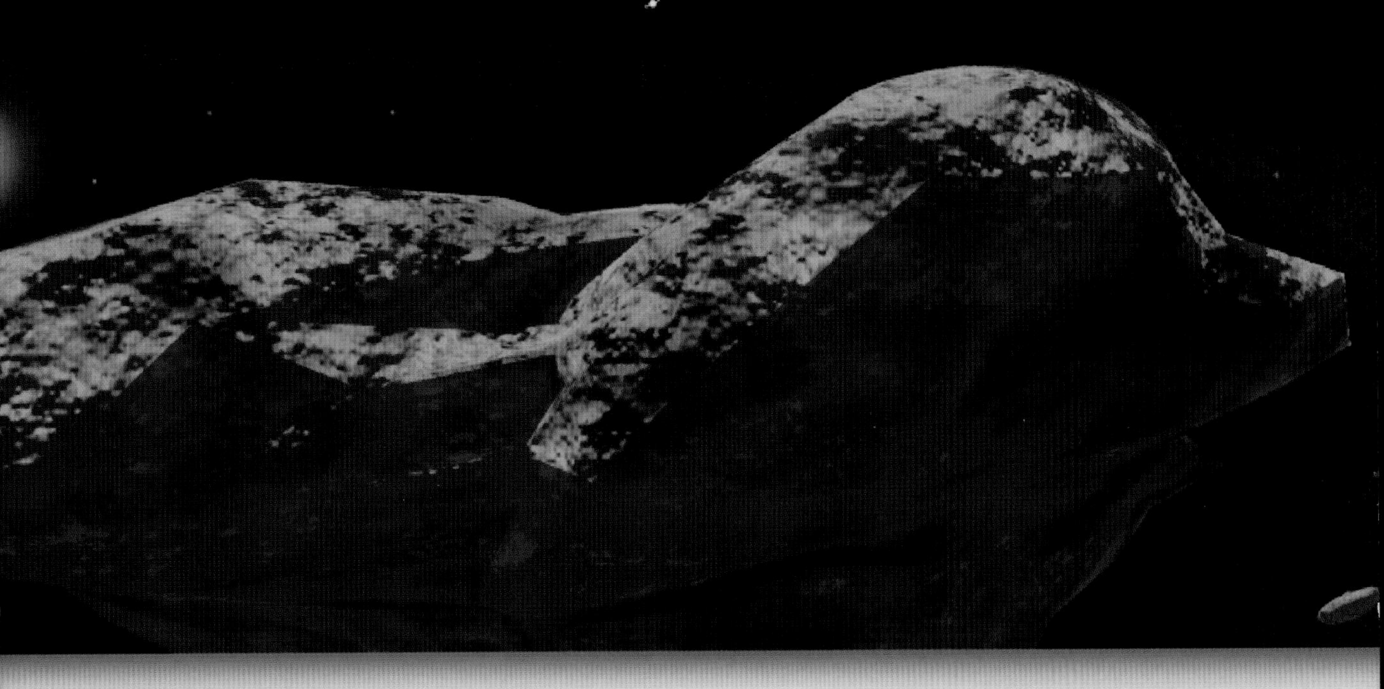

▲ An artist's impression of an asteroid.

Asteroid belts

By 1886, 88 asteroids had been discovered. But as telescopes improved, the numbers of asteroids known increased dramatically. The present asteroid count is over 7,000. It was also discovered that the asteroids formed rings, and that there were gaps between the rings. The gaps in the main asteroid belt—known as Kirkwood gaps—are produced by the **GRAVITATIONAL PULL** of Jupiter. Since the asteroids make their orbits at different speeds than that of Jupiter, they experience different amounts of pull and pushes from different directions of this enormous planet. In time this effect—called resonance—pulls and pushes asteroids into clusters with intervening gaps. Well-known clusters are the Hilda Group, the Thule Group, and the Trojan Group.

ASTEROID Any of the many small objects within the solar system.

ASTEROID BELT The collection of asteroids that orbit the Sun between the orbits of Mars and Jupiter.

COMET A small object, often described as being like a dirty snowball, that appears to be very bright in the night sky and has a long tail when it approaches the Sun.

GRAVITATIONAL PULL The force of attraction between bodies. The larger an object, the more its gravitational pull on other objects.

ORBIT The path followed by one object as it tracks around another.

Eros

▶ The first asteroid found to travel mainly inside the orbit of Mars. It is about 33 km x 13 km.The enlarged picture shows Eros's large, 5.3-kilometer diameter crater.

Some clusters of asteroids have similar patterns of orbit, and they are called families. The three largest families are called Eos, Koronis, and Themis. It is possible that such asteroids were once part of a large body that was shattered in a catastrophic collision. Putting together the pieces gives suggested sizes for the former bodies as 200, 90, and 300 kilometers, respectively.

Similarly, it may be that some of the shattered pieces have been thrown out of orbit, and they are the ones that have Earth-crossing orbits.

Asteroid orbits

Most asteroids orbit the Sun once every 3 to 6 years. Some groups of asteroids cross the orbit of the Earth. The first to be discovered (in 1932) was named the Apollo Group. It is now thought to contain 700 asteroids with a diameter greater than 1 km (and numerous other smaller bodies).

The second group is named the Aten Group. It contains 100 asteroids with a diameter greater than 1 km. The first of them was only discovered in 1976.

A further group is called the Amor Group. It probably contains 1,000 asteroids with a diameter greater than 1 km.

These asteroids are of real and practical interest because as they cross the Earth's path, they must inevitably, from time to time, result in massive collisions.

The most recent near miss was in January 1991, when an Apollo asteroid 10 meters across came as close to the Earth as half the distance between the Earth and the Moon!

Asteroids mostly spin on their **AXES** once every few hours, with an average of 10 hours. The biggest asteroids tend to spin more quickly than the smaller asteroids.

The larger asteroids tend to be spherical (ball-shaped), while the smaller asteroids—which are probably collision debris—are irregular in shape.

The biggest asteroid is Ceres. It has a diameter of about 930 kilometers. Ceres has a **MASS** of about a five-thousandth of the Earth's, but the total mass of all of the asteroids is only three times as much.

Much of the rest of the mass of all asteroids is concentrated in the other large asteroids such as Pallas, which is 535 km across, Vesta, which is 520 km across, and Hygiea, which is 410 km across. There are 26 more with diameters greater than 200 km. In all, there may be 250 asteroids larger than 100 km across. They contain 90% of the entire mass of all of the asteroids. There are probably a million other asteroids more than 1 km across and countless smaller ones.

The largest asteroids—Ceres, Pallas, and Vesta—are big enough to have **GRAVITATIONAL FIELDS** powerful enough to exert a pull on Mars, changing the way it orbits and making it wobble slightly.

Composition

The asteroids are not all made of the same materials. In general they tend to be less dense than the Earth but similar to the Moon. That may be because they have a larger amount of light **MINERALS** and gases than is common on Earth.

Overall, the asteroids seem to be the debris of a tenth planet that never survived the development of the solar system. That would explain why they have different compositions. If the Earth were to break up, its various pieces would also have different compositions, being more dense if they were the remains of the inner regions, and less dense if they were the remains of the **CRUST**.

AXIS (pl. **AXES**) The line around which a body spins.

CRUST The solid outer surface of a rocky body.

GRAVITATIONAL FIELD The region surrounding a body in which that body's gravitational force can be felt.

MASS The amount of matter in an object.

MINERAL A solid crystalline substance.

SATELLITE An object that is in an orbit around another object.

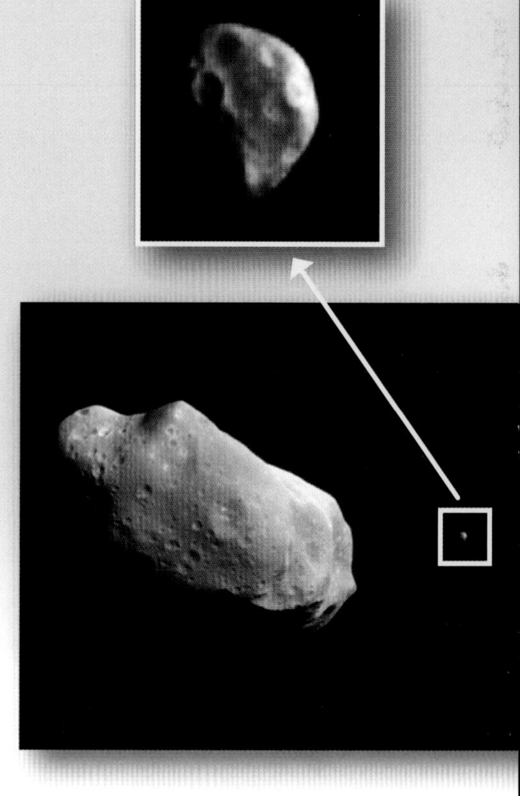

▲ The asteroid Ida has its own **SATELLITE** called Dactyl. Ida's moon is a different color than Ida, although it is believed that it is made of the same basic rock type.

Asteroid collisions

The continuing collisions are probably responsible for putting some asteroids into Earth-crossing orbits, in much the same way as balls are knocked in differing directions after being struck by the cue ball in billiards.

When some of them enter the Earth's atmosphere, they burn up as **METEORS**. But if they are large enough, they strike the ground as **METEORITES**. Large meteorites have produced Meteor Crater in Arizona and other older **CRATERS**. Some people believe that much larger ones were responsible for some rapid changes that have sometimes occurred on the Earth, perhaps causing, for example, periodic mass extinctions of species. The last of them was about 65 million years ago and may have started the change of climate that led to the extinction of the dinosaurs (and many other species). It is thought that an asteroid with a diameter of a kilometer collides with the Earth every million years. Although rare, that doesn't mean it will be another million years before such a collision occurs. That is why scientists are trying to figure out how to send rockets toward possible colliding asteroids and either blow them up or deflect them from their paths.

▲ Meteor Crater (Crater Mound), Arizona.

▼ Comet Borrelly's nucleus, with dust jets escaping and a cloudlike "coma" of dust and gases surrounding it. **FALSE COLOR** has been used to reveal details of the jets and coma.

Borrelly's nucleus is about 8 kilometers from end to end, so the field of view is about 40 kilometers across.

The Sun shines from the bottom of the image. The main dust jet, seen extending toward the bottom left, heads away from the comet in a direction that is about 30° off the direction straight toward the Sun from the comet.

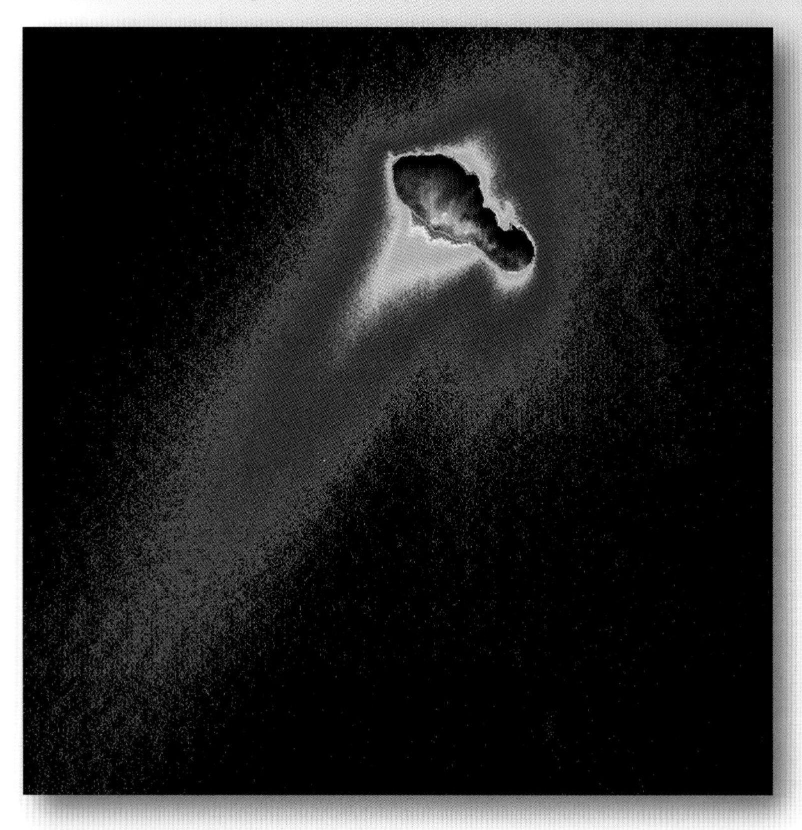

▲ On July 16–22, 1994, over 20 fragments of comet Shoemaker–Levy 9 collided with the planet Jupiter.

The comet was discovered the previous year by astronomers Carolyn and Eugene Shoemaker and David Levy.

Comets

COMETS are small bodies that have very elliptical (or oval-shaped) orbits. The word "comet" comes from the Greek *kometes*, meaning "hairy one." This is a reference to the tail of a comet as seen from the Earth.

The nature of comets

Most comets are very faint and are only found by studying photographs made from telescope observations. The faintest comets that telescopes can detect are about 2 m across.

But although the **NUCLEUS** of a comet is a small, potato-shaped "very dirty snowball"—perhaps 10 or so kilometers across—the **COMA** and tail are gigantic, with a coma typically being 100,000 kilometers across and the tail 100 million kilometers long.

The coma is the dusty "atmosphere" that surrounds the nucleus as the comet approaches the Sun. Together nucleus and coma make the head of the comet. The nucleus continuously feeds the coma and tail, as the **PLASMA** of the coma and tail constantly disappears into the vastness of space.

Although we think of a comet as a white object, in fact the nucleus is pitch black because it contains so much sooty material. What we see is the sparkling **RADIATION** from the coma and the tail.

Most of the surface of the nucleus is the inactive so-called crust. The loss to the coma and tail typically happens from a small number of active zones over the surface. These active zones send out jets of dust. Most of the material leaving the comet is **WATER VAPOR**, along with carbon monoxide and carbon dioxide.

COMA The blurred image caused by light bouncing from a collection of dust and ice particles escaping from the nucleus of a comet.

COMET A small object, often described as being like a dirty snowball, that appears to be very bright in the night sky and has a long tail when it approaches the Sun.

CRATER A deep bowl-shaped depression in the surface of a body formed by the high-speed impact of another, smaller body.

FALSE COLOR The colors used to make the appearance of some property more obvious.

METEOR A streak of light (shooting star) produced by a meteoroid as it enters the Earth's atmosphere.

METEORITE A meteor that reaches the Earth's surface.

NUCLEUS (pl. **NUCLEI**) The centermost part of something, the core.

PLASMA A collection of charged particles that behaves something like a gas. It can conduct an electric charge and be affected by magnetic fields.

RADIATION The transfer of energy in the form of waves (such as light and heat) or particles (such as from radioactive decay of a material).

WATER VAPOR The gaseous form of water. Also sometimes referred to as moisture.

The SOLAR WIND was unknown until in 1951 the German astronomer Ludwig Biermann predicted its existence in order to help explain why a comet's tail always points away from the Sun.

Although we popularly think that all comets have a tail, many, in fact, do not. The tail is mainly a feature of comets relatively close to the Sun when some of the material begins to "burn off" as the solar wind drags gas away from the nucleus. The result is that bluish tail pointing away from the Sun. When comets go far out on their orbits, however, space is so cold that they do not lose any material at all.

▲ An artist's impression of a comet's nucleus and space PROBE Stardust (*top center*). The goal of the Stardust mission, launched in February 1999, is to bring back samples from a comet and INTERSTELLAR dust. From them it is hoped we can learn more about the composition of the early universe.

Comets are made of a combination of "ice" and rock. In this case the "ice" may be solid water or solid methane and solid ammonia. Comets therefore seem to have compositions similar to the gas giant planets.

The origins of life on Earth?

Comets still contain unchanged the material from which the solar system was made. This material includes ATOMS of hydrogen, carbon, oxygen, nitrogen, and sulfur. From them it is possible to make ORGANIC MATERIALS. It is also possible that comets contain larger MOLECULES such as AMINO ACIDS. For this reason some scientists believe that comets could well be the link between outer space and life on Earth.

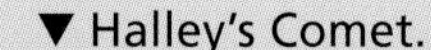

▼ Halley's Comet.

Where comets come from

It is likely that comets were all part of the early solar system and were not captured by the larger planets. Instead of attracting them, the GRAVITATIONAL FIELD of the planets flung them out from the Sun in a kind of "slingshot" effect (the effect used to ACCELERATE spacecraft from one planet to another, see page 14).

Some left the solar system forever, while about 10 trillion remained in a great cloud named the **OORT CLOUD** after the Dutch astronomer Jan Hendrik Oort. The Oort cloud lies outside what we normally think of as the solar system, but it is still gravitationally held to it. It is our permanent source of comets.

The comets still in the Oort cloud do not have comas or tails, and so they remain as dark objects in the sky, completely invisible to us.

The return period of a comet

To many people Sir Edmund Halley is most famously connected with comets. In his pioneering studies of the paths of comets he used calculations by Sir Isaac Newton to show that a comet moved in an ellipse (an oval). The first comet that returned to view following these predictions was observed in 1758 and became known as Halley's Comet.

Halley's Comet returns irregularly to within sight, but averages 76 years. The variability depends on how close the comet comes to Jupiter, whose gravity alters its path and therefore the return period of the comet.

Many comets have return periods that are on the order of thousands of years or more. Halley's Comet is the only bright comet that returns within the span of a human lifetime.

It is believed that comets only survive a few hundred revolutions on their ellipses—and therefore last less than a million years—before they burn away.

Meteoroids, meteors, and meteorites

METEOROIDS are any small space objects that cross the path of the Earth. Using this definition, asteroids are meteoroids if they cross the path of the Earth.

METEORS are any small space particles that are made visible as they burn up on entering the Earth's atmosphere. They are usually no more than specks of sand-sized material, but can be as large as pebbles. If they reach the Earth's surface without completely burning up, the rocky body on the ground is called a meteorite.

ACCELERATE To gain speed.

AMINO ACIDS Simple organic molecules that can be building blocks for living things.

ATOM The smallest particle of an element.

GRAVITATIONAL FIELD The region surrounding a body in which that body's gravitational force can be felt.

INTERSTELLAR Between the stars.

METEOR A streak of light (shooting star) produced by a meteoroid as it enters the Earth's atmosphere.

METEOROID A small body moving in the solar system that becomes a meteor if it enters the Earth's atmosphere.

MOLECULE A group of two or more atoms held together by chemical bonds.

OORT CLOUD A region on the edge of the solar system that consists of planetesimals and comets that did not get caught up in planet making.

ORGANIC MATERIAL Any matter that contains carbon and is alive.

PROBE An unmanned spacecraft designed to explore our solar system and beyond.

SOLAR WIND The flow of tiny charged particles (called plasma) outward from the Sun.

As meteors fly through the air, their high speed gives rise to a SONIC BOOM, just as a supersonic aircraft does. Some meteorites weigh several tonnes.

Two kinds of meteorite are found: stony meteorites that are made of silicate minerals, and iron meteorites made of nickel and iron. They are believed to be mostly the remnants of former planets that have broken up as a result of some earlier collision. Most meteoroids therefore come from the asteroid belt. However, collisions of meteoroids with both the Moon and Mars have caused pieces of these bodies to be broken off and hurled into space, finally falling to Earth as meteors.

Chance collisions

There are streams of meteors in space orbiting in well-known patterns, often similar to some comets and perhaps particles from the comets as they disintegrate. It is as though the comets were leaving behind a trail of dust whose particles continued to orbit at their own speed with the comet traveling through them. Because they are found in the entire cometary orbit, the Earth passes through them much more often than it sees the comet, with the result that meteor showers (shooting stars, fireballs) can be predicted and seen on known dates.

Meteoroids bigger than 100 m across do not burn up entirely and strike the ground at speeds of several kilometers a second, making large impact craters. Such impacts on bodies without an atmosphere, such as the Moon, create much of the cratered surface.

The largest recent meteor struck Earth on June 30, 1908, in the Tunguska region of central Siberia. At the time people reported that it was as bright as the Sun. Its impact gave out as much energy as a 10 megaton bomb. But the size of some geological craters suggests that in the past, some have struck with impacts equivalent to 100 million megatons.

KUIPER BELT A belt of planetesimals (small rocky bodies, one kilometer to hundreds of kilometers across) much closer to the Sun than the Oort cloud.

SONIC BOOM The noise created when an object moves faster than the speed of sound.

◀ Artist's impression of the *New Horizons* spacecraft encountering a KUIPER BELT object (meteoroid). The Sun is more than 6.7 billion kilometers away and shines no more than a bright star. Jupiter and Neptune are visible as orange and blue "stars" to the right of the Sun.

New Horizons is due for launch in January 2006 and should reach Pluto and Charon 9 years later in 2015.

SET GLOSSARY

Metric (SI) and U.S. standard unit conversion table

1 kilometer = 0.6 mile
1 meter = 3.3 feet or 1.1 yards
1 centimeter = 0.4 inch
1 tonne = (metric ton) 1,000 kilograms, or 2,204.6 pounds
1 kilogram = 2.2 pounds
1 gram = 0.035 ounces

1 mile = 1.6 kilometers
1 foot = 0.3 meter
1 inch = 25.4 millimeters or 2.54 centimeters
1 ton = 907.18 kilograms in standard units, 1,016.05 kilograms in metric
1 pound = 0.45 kilograms
1 ounce = 28 grams

0°C = 5/9 (32°F)

ABSOLUTE ZERO The coldest possible temperature, defined as 0 K or –273°C.
See also: **K.**

ACCELERATE To gain speed.

AERODYNAMIC A shape offering as little resistance to the air as possible.

AIR RESISTANCE The frictional drag that an object creates as it moves rapidly through the air.

AMINO ACIDS Simple organic molecules that can be building blocks for living things.

ANNULAR Ringlike.
An annular eclipse occurs when the dark disk of the Moon does not completely obscure the Sun.

ANTENNA (pl. ANTENNAE) A device, often in the shape of a rod or wire, used for sending out and receiving radio waves.

ANTICLINE An arching fold of rock layers where the rocks slope down from the crest.

ANTICYCLONE A roughly circular region of the atmosphere that is spiraling outward and downward.

APOGEE The point on an orbit where the orbiting object is at its farthest from the object it is orbiting.

APOLLO The program developed in the United States by NASA to get people to the Moon's surface and back safely.

ARRAY A regular group or arrangement.

ASH Fragments of lava that have cooled and solidified between when they leave a volcano and when they fall to the surface.

ASTEROID Any of the many small objects within the solar system.
Asteroids are rocky or metallic and are conventionally described as significant bodies with a diameter smaller than 1,000 km. Asteroids mainly occupy a belt between Mars and Jupiter (asteroid belt).

ASTEROID BELT The collection of asteroids that orbit the Sun between the orbits of Mars and Jupiter.

ASTHENOSPHERE The region below the lithosphere, and therefore part of the upper mantle, in which some material may be molten.

ASTRONOMICAL UNIT (AU) The average distance from the Earth to the Sun (149,597,870 km).

ASTRONOMY The study of space beyond the Earth and its contents. It includes those phenomena that affect the Earth but that originate in space, such as meteorites and aurora.

ASTROPHYSICS The study of physics in space, what other stars, galaxies, and planets are like, and the physical laws that govern them.

ASYNCHRONOUS Not connected in time or pace.

ATMOSPHERE The envelope of gases that surrounds the Earth and other bodies in the universe.
The Earth's atmosphere is very different from that of other planets, being, for example, far lower in hydrogen and helium than the gas giants and lower in carbon dioxide than Venus, but richer in oxygen than all the others.

ATMOSPHERIC PRESSURE The pressure on the gases in the atmosphere caused by gravity pulling them toward the center of a celestial body.

ATOM The smallest particle of an element.

ATOMIC MASS UNIT A measure of the mass of an atom or molecule.
An atomic mass unit equals one-twelfth of the mass of an atom of carbon-12.

ATOMIC WEAPONS Weapons that rely on the violent explosive force achieved when radioactive materials are made to go into an uncontrollable chain reaction.

ATOMIC WEIGHT The ratio of the average mass of a chemical element's atoms to carbon-12.

AURORA A region of illumination, often in the form of a wavy curtain, high in the atmosphere of a planet.
It is the result of the interaction of the planet's magnetic field with the particles in the solar wind. High-energy electrons from the solar wind race along the planet's magnetic field into the upper atmosphere. The electrons excite atmospheric gases, making them glow.

AXIS (pl. AXES) The line around which a body spins.
The Earth spins around an axis through its north and south geographic poles.

BALLISTIC MISSILE A rocket that is guided up in a high arching path; then the fuel supply is cut, and it is allowed to fall to the ground.

BASIN A large depression in the ground (bigger than a crater).

BIG BANG The theory that the universe as we know it started from a single point (called a singularity) and then exploded outward. It is still expanding today.

BINARY STAR A pair of stars that are gravitationally attracted, and that revolve around one another.

BLACK DWARF A degenerate star that has cooled so that it is now not visible.

BLACK HOLE An object that has a gravitational pull so strong that nothing can escape from it.
A black hole may have a mass equal to thousands of stars or more.

BLUE GIANT A young, extremely bright and hot star of very large mass that has used up all its hydrogen and is no longer in the main sequence. When a blue giant ages, it becomes a red giant.

BOILING POINT The change of state of a substance in which a liquid rapidly turns into a gas without a change in temperature.

BOOSTER POD A form of housing that stands outside the main body of the launcher.

CALDERA A large pit in the top of a volcano produced when the top of the volcano explodes and collapses in on itself.

CAPSULE A small pressurized space vehicle.

CATALYST A substance that speeds up a chemical reaction but that is itself unchanged.

CELESTIAL Relating to the sky above, the "heavens."

CENTER OF GRAVITY The point at which all of the mass of an object can be balanced.

CENTRIFUGAL FORCE A force that acts on an orbiting or spinning body, tending to oppose gravity and move away from the center of rotation.
For orbiting objects the centrifugal force acts in the opposite direction from gravity. When satellites orbit the Earth, the centrifugal force balances out the force of gravity.

CENTRIFUGE An instrument for spinning small samples very rapidly.

CHAIN REACTION A sequence of related events with one event triggering the next.

CHASM A deep, narrow trench.

CHROMOSPHERE The shell of gases that makes up part of the atmosphere of a star and lies between the photosphere and the corona.

CIRCUMFERENCE The distance around the edge of a circle or sphere.

COMA The blurred image caused by light bouncing from a collection of dust and ice particles escaping from the nucleus of a comet.

The coma changes the appearance of a comet from a point source of reflective light to a blurry object with a tail.

COMBUSTION CHAMBER A vessel inside an engine or motor where the fuel components mix and are set on fire, that is, they are burned (combusted).

COMET A small object, often described as being like a dirty snowball, that appears to be very bright in the night sky and has a long tail when it approaches the Sun.

Comets are thought to be some of the oldest objects in the solar system.

COMPLEMENTARY COLOR A color that is diametrically opposed in the range, or circle, of colors in the spectrum; for example, cyan (blue) is the complement of red.

COMPOSITE A material made from solid threads in a liquid matrix that is allowed to set.

COMPOUND A substance made from two or more elements that have chemically combined.

Ammonia is an example of a compound made from the elements hydrogen and nitrogen.

CONDENSE/CONDENSATION (1) To make something more concentrated or compact.

(2) The change of state from a gas or vapor to a liquid.

CONDUCTION The transfer of heat between two objects when they touch.

CONSTELLATION One of many commonly recognized patterns of stars in the sky.

CONVECTION/CONVECTION CURRENTS The circulating flow in a fluid (liquid or gas) that occurs when it is heated from below.

Convective flow is caused in a fluid by the tendency for hotter, and therefore less dense, material to rise and for colder, and therefore more dense, material, to sink with gravity. That results in a heat transfer.

CORE The central region of a body.

The core of the Earth is about 3,300 km in radius, compared with the radius of the whole Earth, which is 6,300 km.

CORONA (pl. **CORONAE**) (1) A colored circle seen around a bright object such as a star.

(2) The gases surrounding a star such as the Sun. In the case of the Sun and certain other stars these gases are extremely hot.

(3) A circular to oval pattern of faults, fractures, and ridges with a sagging center as found on Venus. In the case of Venus they are a few hundred kilometers in diameter.

CORONAL MASS EJECTIONS Very large bubbles of plasma escaping into the corona.

CORROSIVE SUBSTANCE Something that chemically eats away something else.

COSMOLOGICAL PRINCIPLE States that the way you see the universe is independent of the place where you are (your location). In effect, it means that the universe is roughly uniform throughout.

COSMONAUT A Russian space person.

COSMOS The universe and everything in it. The word "cosmos" suggests that the universe operates according to orderly principles.

CRATER A deep bowl-shaped depression in the surface of a body formed by the high-speed impact of another, smaller body.

Most craters are formed by the impact of asteroids and meteoroids. Craters have both a depression, or pit, and also an elevated rim formed of the material displaced from the central pit.

CRESCENT The appearance of the Moon when it is between a new Moon and a half Moon.

CRUST The solid outer surface of a rocky body.

The crust of the Earth is mainly just a few tens of kilometers thick, compared to the total radius of 6,300 km for the whole Earth. It forms much of the lithosphere.

CRYSTAL An ordered arrangement of molecules in a compound. Crystals that grow freely develop flat surfaces.

CYCLONE A large storm in which the atmosphere spirals inward and upward.

On Earth cyclones have a very low atmospheric pressure at their center and often contain deep clouds.

DARK MATTER Matter that does not shine or reflect light.

No one has ever found dark matter, but it is thought to exist because the amount of ordinary matter in the universe is not enough to account for many gravitational effects that have been observed.

DENSITY A measure of the amount of matter in a space.

Density is often measured in grams per cubic centimeter. The density of the Earth is 5.5 grams per cubic centimeter.

DEORBIT To move out of an orbital position and begin a reentry path toward the Earth.

DEPRESSION (1) A sunken area or hollow in a surface or landscape.

(2) A region of inward swirling air in the atmosphere associated with cloudy weather and rain.

DIFFRACTION The bending of light as it goes through materials of different density.

DISK A shape or surface that looks round and flat.

DOCK To meet with and attach to another space vehicle.

DOCKING PORT/STATION A place on the side of a spacecraft that contains some form of anchoring mechanism and an airlock.

DOPPLER EFFECT The apparent change in pitch of a fast-moving object as it approaches or leaves an observer.

DOWNLINK A communication to Earth from a spacecraft.

DRAG A force that hinders the movement of something.

DWARF STAR A star that shines with a brightness that is average or below.

EARTH The third planet from the Sun and the one on which we live.

The Earth belongs to the group of rocky planets. It is unique in having an oxygen-rich atmosphere and water, commonly found in its three phases—solid, liquid, and gas.

EARTHQUAKE The shock waves produced by the sudden movement of two pieces of brittle crust.

ECCENTRIC A noncircular, or oval, orbit.

ECLIPSE The time when light is cut off by a body coming between the observer and the source of the illumination (for example, eclipse of the Sun), or when the body the observer is on comes between the source of illumination and another body (for example, eclipse of the Moon).

It happens when three bodies are in a line. This phenomenon is not necessarily called an eclipse. Occultations of stars by the Moon and transits of Venus or Mercury are examples of different expressions used instead of "eclipse."

See also: **TOTAL ECLIPSE.**

ECOLOGY The study of living things in their environment.

ELECTRONS Negatively charged particles that are parts of atoms.

ELEMENT A substance that cannot be decomposed into simpler substances by chemical means.

Elements are the building blocks of compounds. For example, silicon and oxygen are elements. They combine to form the compound silicon dioxide, or quartz.

ELLIPTICAL GALAXY A galaxy that has an oval shape rather like a football, and that has no spiral arms.

EL NIÑO A time when ocean currents in the Pacific Ocean reverse from their normal pattern and disrupt global weather patterns. It occurs once every 4 or 5 years.

EMISSION Something that is sent or let out.

ENCKE GAP A gap between rings around Saturn named for the astronomer Johann Franz Encke (1791–1865).

EPOXY RESIN Adhesives that develop their strength as they react, or "cure," after mixing.

EQUATOR The ring drawn around a body midway between the poles.

EQUILIBRIUM A state of balance.

ESA The European Space Agency. ESA is an organizaton of European countries for cooperation in space research and technology. It operates several installations around Europe and has its headquarters in Paris, France.

ESCARPMENT A sharp-edged ridge.

EVAPORATE/EVAPORATION The change in state from liquid to a gas.

EXOSPHERE The outer part of the atmosphere starting about 500 km from the surface. This layer contains so little air that molecules rarely collide.

EXTRAVEHICULAR ACTIVITY Any task performed by people outside the protected environment of a space vehicle's pressurized compartments. Extravehicular activities (EVA) include repairing equipment in the Space Shuttle bay.

FALSE COLOR The colors used to make the appearance of some property more obvious.

They are part of the computer generation of an image.

FAULT A place in the crust where rocks have fractured, and then one side has moved relative to the other.

A fault is caused by excessive pressure on brittle rocks.

FLUORESCENT Emitting the visible light produced by a substance when it is struck by invisible waves, such as ultraviolet waves.

FRACTURE A break in brittle rock.

FREQUENCY The number of complete cycles of (for example, radio) waves received per second.

FRICTION The force that resists two bodies that are in contact.

For example, the effect of the ocean waters moving as tides slows the Earth's rotation.

FUSION The joining of atomic nuclei to form heavier nuclei.

This process results in the release of huge amounts of energy.

GALAXY A system of stars and interstellar matter within the universe.

Galaxies may contain billions of stars.

GALILEAN SATELLITES The four large satellites of Jupiter discovered by astronomer Galileo Galilei in 1610. They are Callisto, Europa, Ganymede, and Io.

GALILEO A U.S. space probe launched in October 1989 and designed for intensive investigation of Jupiter.

GEIGER TUBE A device to detect radioactive materials.

GEOSTATIONARY ORBIT A circular orbit 35,786 km directly above the Earth's equator.

Communications satellites frequently use this orbit. A satellite in a geostationary orbit will move at the same rate as the Earth's rotation, completing one revolution in 24 hours. That way it remains at the same point over the Earth's equator.

GEOSTATIONARY SATELLITE A man-made satellite in a fixed or geosynchronous orbit around the Earth.

GEOSYNCHRONOUS ORBIT An orbit in which a satellite makes one circuit of the Earth in 24 hours.

A geosynchronous orbit coincides with the Earth's orbit—it takes the same time to complete an orbit as it does for the Earth to make one complete rotation. If the orbit is circular and above the equator, then the satellite remains over one particular point of the equator; that is called a geostationary orbit.

GEOSYNCLINE A large downward sag or trench that forms in the Earth's crust as a result of colliding tectonic plates.

GEYSER A periodic fountain of material. On Earth geysers are of water and steam, but on other planets and moons they are formed from other substances, for example, nitrogen gas on Triton.

GIBBOUS When between half and a full disk of a body can be seen lighted by the Sun.

GIMBALS A framework that allows anything inside it to move in a variety of directions.

GLOBAL POSITIONING SYSTEM A network of geostationary satellites that can be used to locate the position of any object on the Earth's surface.

GRANULATION The speckled pattern we see in the Sun's photosphere as a result of convectional overturning of gases.

GRAVITATIONAL FIELD The region surrounding a body in which that body's gravitational force can be felt.

The gravitational field of the Sun spreads over the entire solar system. The gravitational fields of the planets each exert some influence on the orbits of their neighbors.

GRAVITY/GRAVITATIONAL FORCE/ GRAVITATIONAL PULL The force of attraction between bodies. The larger an object, the more its gravitational pull on other objects.

The Sun's gravity is the most powerful in the solar system, keeping all of the planets and other materials within the solar system.

GREAT RED SPOT A large, almost permanent feature of the Jovian atmosphere that moves around the planet at about latitude 23°S.

GREENHOUSE EFFECT The increase in atmospheric temperature produced by the presence of carbon dioxide in the air.

Carbon dioxide has the ability to soak up heat radiated from the surface of a planet and partly prevent its escape. The effect is similar to that produced by a greenhouse.

GROUND STATION A receiving and transmitting station in direct communication with satellites. Such stations are characterized by having large dish-shaped antennae.

GULLY (pl. **GULLIES**) A trench in the land surface formed, on Earth, by running water.

GYROSCOPE A device in which a rapidly spinning wheel is held in a frame in such a way that it can rotate in any direction. The momentum of the wheel means that the gyroscope retains its position even when the frame is tilted.

HEAT SHIELD A protective device on the outside of a space vehicle that absorbs the heat during reentry and protects it from burning up.

HELIOPAUSE The edge of the heliosphere.

HELIOSEISMOLOGY The study of the internal structure of the Sun by modeling the Sun's patterns of internal shock waves.

HELIOSPHERE The entire range of influence of the Sun. It extends to the edge of the solar system.

HUBBLE SPACE TELESCOPE An orbiting telescope (and so a satellite) that was placed above the Earth's atmosphere so that it could take images that were far clearer than anything that could be obtained from the surface of the Earth.

HURRICANE A very violent cyclone that begins close to the equator, and that contains winds of over 117 km/hr.

ICE CAP A small mountainous region that is covered in ice.

INFRARED Radiation with a wavelength that is longer than red light.

INNER PLANETS The rocky planets closest to the Sun. They are Mercury, Venus, Earth, and Mars.

INTERNATIONAL SPACE STATION The international orbiting space laboratory.

INTERPLANETARY DUST The fine dustlike material that lies scattered through space, and that exists between the planets as well as in outer space.

INTERSTELLAR Between the stars.

IONIZED Matter that has been converted into small charged particles called ions.

An atom that has gained or lost an electron.

IONOSPHERE A part of the Earth's atmosphere in which the number of ions (electrically charged particles) is enough to affect how radio waves move.

The ionosphere begins about 50 km above the Earth's surface.

IRREGULAR SATELLITES Satellites that orbit in the opposite direction from their parent planet.

This motion is also called retrograde rotation.

ISOTOPE Atoms that have the same number of protons in their nucleus, but that have different masses; for example, carbon-12 and carbon-14.

JOVIAN PLANETS An alternative group name for the gas giant planets: Jupiter, Saturn, Uranus, and Neptune.

JUPITER The fifth planet from the Sun and two planets farther away from the Sun than the Earth.

Jupiter is 318 times as massive as the Earth and 1,500 times as big by volume. It is the largest of the gas giants.

K Named for British scientist Lord Kelvin (1824–1907), it is a measurement of absolute temperature. Zero K is called absolute zero and is only approached in deep space: ice melts at 273 K, and water boils at 373 K.

KEELER GAP A gap in the rings of Saturn named for the astronomer James Edward Keeler (1857–1900).

KILOPARSEC A unit of a thousand parsecs. A parsec is the unit used for measuring the largest distances in the universe.

KUIPER BELT A belt of planetesimals (small rocky bodies, one kilometer to hundreds of kilometers across) much closer to the Sun than the Oort cloud.

LANDSLIDE A sudden collapse of material on a steep slope.

LA NIÑA Below normal ocean temperatures in the eastern Pacific Ocean that disrupt global weather patterns.

LATITUDE Angular distance north or south of the equator, measured through 90°.

LAUNCH VEHICLE/LAUNCHER A system of propellant tanks and rocket motors or engines designed to lift a payload into space. It may, or may not, be part of a space vehicle.

LAVA Hot, melted rock from a volcano.

Lava flows onto the surface of a planet and cools and hardens to form new rock. Most of the lava on Earth is made of basalt.

LAVA FLOW A river or sheet of liquid volcanic rock.

LAWS OF MOTION Formulated by Sir Isaac Newton, they describe the forces that act on a moving object.

The first law states that an object will keep moving in a straight line at constant speed unless it is acted on by a force.

The second law states that the force on an object is related to the mass of the object multiplied by its acceleration.

The third law states that an action always has an equal and directly opposite reaction.

LIFT An upthrust on the wing of a plane that occurs when it moves rapidly through the air. It is the main way of suspending an airplane during flight. The engines simply provide the forward thrust.

LIGHT-YEAR The distance traveled by light through space in one Earth year, or 63,240 astronomical units.

The speed of light is the speed that light travels through a vacuum, which is 299,792 km/s.

LIMB The outer edge of a celestial body, including an atmosphere if it has one.

LITHOSPHERE The upper part of the Earth, corresponding generally to the crust and believed to be about 80 km thick.

LOCAL GROUP The Milky Way, the Magellanic Clouds, the Andromeda Galaxy, and over 20 other relatively near galaxies.

LUNAR Anything to do with the Moon.

MAGELLANIC CLOUD Either of two small galaxies that are companions to the Milky Way Galaxy.

MAGMA Hot, melted rock inside the Earth that, when cooled, forms igneous rock.

Magma is associated with volcanic activity.

MAGNETIC FIELD The region of influence of a magnetic body.

The Earth's magnetic field stretches out beyond the atmosphere into space. There it interacts with the solar wind to produce auroras.

MAGNETISM An invisible force that has the property of attracting iron and similar metals.

MAGNETOPAUSE The outer edge of the magnetosphere.

MAGNETOSPHERE A region in the upper atmosphere, or around a planet, where magnetic phenomena such as auroras are found.

MAGNITUDE A measure of the brightness of a star.

The apparent magnitude is the brightness of a celestial object as seen from the Earth. The absolute magnitude is the standardized brightness measured as though all objects were the same distance from the Earth. The brighter the object, the lower its magnitude number. For example, a star of magnitude 4 is 2.5 times as bright as one of magnitude 5. A difference of five magnitudes is the same as a difference in brightness of 100 to 1. The brightest stars have negative numbers. The Sun's apparent magnitude is –26.8. Its absolute magnitude is 4.8.

MAIN SEQUENCE The 90% of stars in the universe that represent the mature phase of stars with small or medium mass.

MANTLE The region of a planet between the core and the crust.

The Earth's mantle is about 2,900 km thick, and its upper surface may be molten in some places.

MARE (pl. **MARIA**) A flat, dark plain created by lava flows. They were once thought to be seas.

MARS The fourth planet from the Sun in our solar system and one planet farther away from the Sun than the Earth.

Mars is a rocky planet almost half the diameter of Earth that is a distinctive rust-red color.

MASCON A region of higher surface density on the Moon.

MASS The amount of matter in an object.

The amount of matter, and so the mass, remains the same, but the effect of gravity gives the mass a weight. The weight depends on the gravitational pull. Thus a ball will have the same mass on the Earth and on the Moon, but it will weigh a sixth as much on the Moon because the force of gravity there is only a sixth as strong.

MATTER Anything that exists in physical form.

Everything we can see is made of matter. The building blocks of matter are atoms.

MERCURY The closest planet to the Sun in our solar system and two planets closer to the Sun than Earth.

Mercury is a gray-colored rocky planet less than half the diameter of Earth. It has the most extreme temperature range of any planet in our solar system.

MESOSPHERE One of the upper regions of the atmosphere, beginning at the top of the stratosphere and continuing from 50 km upward until the temperature stops declining.

METEOR A streak of light (shooting star) produced by a meteoroid as it enters the Earth's atmosphere.

The friction with the Earth's atmosphere causes the small body to glow (become incandescent). That is what we see as a streak of light.

METEORITE A meteor that reaches the Earth's surface.

METEOROID A small body moving in the solar system that becomes a meteor if it enters the Earth's atmosphere.

Meteoroids are typically only a few millimeters across and burn up as they go through the atmosphere, but some have crashed to the Earth, making large craters.

MICROMETEORITES Tiny pieces of space dust moving at high speeds.

MICRON A millionth of a meter.

MICROWAVELENGTH Waves at the shortest end of the radio wavelengths.

MICROWAVE RADIATION The background radiation that is found everywhere in space, and whose existence is used to support the Big Bang theory.

MILKY WAY The spiral galaxy in which our star and solar system are situated.

MINERAL A solid crystalline substance.

MINOR PLANET Another term for an asteroid.

M NUMBER In 1781 Charles Messier began a catalogue of the objects he could see in the night sky. He gave each of them a unique number. The first entry was called M1. There is no significance to the number in terms of brightness, size, closeness, or otherwise.

MODULE A section, or part, of a space vehicle.

MOLECULE A group of two or more atoms held together by chemical bonds.

MOLTEN Liquid, suggesting that it has changed from a solid.

MOMENTUM The mass of an object multiplied by its velocity.

MOON The natural satellite that orbits the Earth.

Other planets have large satellites, or moons, but none is relatively as large as our Moon, suggesting that it has a unique origin.

MOON The name generally given to any large natural satellite of a planet.

MOUNTAIN RANGE A long, narrow region of very high land that contains several or many mountains.

NASA The National Aeronautics and Space Administration.

NASA was founded in 1958 for aeronautical and space exploration. It operates several installations around the country and has its headquarters in Washington, D.C.

NEAP TIDE A tide showing the smallest difference between high and low tides.

NEBULA (pl. **NEBULAE**) Clouds of gas and dust that exist in the space between stars.

The word means mist or cloud and is also used as an alternative to galaxy. The gas makes up to 5% of the mass of a galaxy. What a nebula looks like depends on the arrangement of gas and dust within it.

NEPTUNE The eighth planet from the Sun in our solar system and five planets farther away from the Sun than the Earth.

Neptune is a gas planet that is almost four times the diameter of Earth. It is blue.

NEUTRINOS An uncharged fundamental particle that is thought to have no mass.

NEUTRONS Particles inside the core of an atom that are neutral (have no charge).

NEUTRON STAR A very dense star that consists only of tightly packed neutrons. It is the result of the collapse of a massive star.

NOBLE GASES The unreactive gases, such as neon, xenon, and krypton.

NOVA (pl. **NOVAE**) (1) A star that suddenly becomes much brighter, then fades away to its original brightness within a few months. *See also:* **SUPERNOVA.**

(2) A radiating pattern of faults and fractures unique to Venus.

NUCLEAR DEVICES Anything that is powered by a source of radioactivity.

NUCLEUS (pl. **NUCLEI**) The centermost part of something, the core.

OORT CLOUD A region on the edge of the solar system that consists of planetesimals and comets that did not get caught up in planet making.

OPTICAL Relating to the use of light.

ORBIT The path followed by one object as it tracks around another.

The orbits of the planets around the Sun and moons around their planets are oval, or elliptical.

ORGANIC MATERIAL Any matter that contains carbon and is alive.

OUTER PLANETS The gas giant planets Jupiter, Saturn, Uranus, and Neptune plus the rocky planet Pluto.

OXIDIZER The substance in a reaction that removes electrons from and thereby oxidizes (burns) another substance.

In the case of oxygen this results in the other substance combining with the oxygen to form an oxide (also called an oxidizing agent).

OZONE A form of oxygen (O_3) with three atoms in each molecule instead of the more usual two (O_2).

OZONE HOLE The observed lack of the gas ozone in the upper atmosphere.

PARSEC The unit used for measuring the largest distances in the universe.

A parsec is the distance at which an observer in space would see the radius of the orbit as making one second of arc. This gives a distance of about 3.26 light-years.

See also: **KILOPARSEC.**

PAYLOAD The spacecraft that is carried into space by a launcher.

PENUMBRA (1) A region that is in semidarkness during an eclipse.

(2) The part of a sunspot surrounding the umbra.

PERCOLATE To flow by gravity between particles, for example, of soil.

PERIGEE The point on an orbit where the orbiting object is as close as it ever comes to the object it is orbiting.

PHARMACEUTICAL Relating to medicinal drugs.

PHASE The differing appearance of a body that is closer to the Sun, and that is illuminated by it.

PHOTOCHEMICAL SMOG A hazy atmosphere, often brown, resulting from the reaction of nitrogen gases with sunlight.

PHOTOMOSAIC A composite picture made up of several other pictures that individually only cover a small area.

PHOTON A particle (quantum) of electromagnetic radiation.

PHOTOSPHERE A shell of the Sun that we regard as its visible surface.

PHOTOSYNTHESIS The process that plants use to combine the substances in the environment, such as carbon dioxide, minerals, and water, with oxygen and energy-rich organic compounds by using the energy of sunlight.

PIONEER A name for a series of unmanned U.S. spacecraft.

Pioneer 1 was launched into lunar orbit on October 11, 1958. The others all went into deep space.

PLAIN A flat or gently rolling part of a landscape.

Plains are confined to lowlands. If a flat surface exists in an upland, it is called a plateau.

PLANE A flat surface.

PLANET Any of the large bodies that orbit the Sun.

The planets are (outward from the Sun): Mercury, Venus, Earth, Mars, Jupiter, Saturn, Uranus, Neptune, and Pluto. The rocky planets all have densities greater than 3 grams per cubic centimeter; the gaseous ones less than 2 grams per cubic centimeter.

PLANETARY NEBULA A compact ring or oval nebula that is made of material thrown out of a hot star.

The term "planetary nebula" is a misnomer; dying stars create these cocoons when they lose outer layers of gas. The process has nothing to do with planet formation, which is predicted to happen early in a star's life.

The term originates from a time when people, looking through weak telescopes, thought that the nebulae resembled planets within the solar system, when in fact they were expanding shells of glowing gas in far-off galaxies.

PLANETESIMAL Small rocky bodies one kilometer to hundreds of kilometers across.

The word especially relates to materials that exist in the early stages of the formation of a star and its planets from the dust of a nebula, which will eventually group together to form planets. Some are rock, others a mixture of rock and ice.

PLANKTON Microscopic creatures that float in water.

PLASMA A collection of charged particles that behaves something like a gas. It can conduct an electric charge and be affected by magnetic fields.

PLASTIC The ability of certain solid substances to be molded or deformed to a new shape under pressure without cracking.

PLATE A very large unbroken part of the crust of a planet. Also called tectonic plate.

On Earth the tectonic plates are dragged across the surface by convection currents in the underlying mantle.

PLATEAU An upland plain or tableland.

PLUTO The ninth planet from the Sun and six planets farther from the Sun than the Earth.

Pluto is one of the rocky planets, but it is very different from the others, perhaps being a mixture of rock and ice. It is about two-thirds the size of our Moon.

POLE The geographic pole is the place where a line drawn along the axis of rotation exits from a body's surface.

Magnetic poles do not always correspond with geographic poles.

POLYMER A compound that is made up of long chains formed by combining molecules called monomers as repeating units. ("Poly" means many, "mer" means part.)

PRESSURE The force per unit area.

PROBE An unmanned spacecraft designed to explore our solar system and beyond.

Voyager, Cassini, and Magellan are examples of probes.

PROJECTILE An object propelled through the air or space by an external force or an on-board engine.

PROMINENCE A cloud of burning ionized gas that rises through the Sun's chromosphere into the corona. It can take the form of a sheet or a loop.

PROPELLANT A gas, liquid, or solid that can be expelled rapidly from the end of an object in order to give it motion.

Liquefied gases and solids are used as rocket propellants.

PROPULSION SYSTEM The motors or rockets and their tanks designed to give a launcher or space vehicle the thrust it needs.

PROTEIN Molecules in living things that are vital for building tissues.

PROTONS Positively charged particles from the core of an atom.

PROTOSTAR A cloud of gas and dust that begins to swirl around; the resulting gravity gives birth to a star.

PULSAR A neutron star that is spinning around, releasing electromagnetic radiation, including radio waves.

QUANTUM THEORY A concept of how energy can be divided into tiny pieces called quanta, which is the key to how the smallest particles work and how they build together to make the universe around us.

QUASAR A rare starlike object of enormous brightness that gives out radio waves, which are thought to be released as material is sucked toward a black hole.

RADAR Short for radio detecting and ranging. A system of bouncing radio waves from objects in order to map their surfaces and find out how far away they are.

Radar is useful in conditions where visible light cannot be used.

RADIATION/RADIATE The transfer of energy in the form of waves (such as light and heat) or particles (such as from radioactive decay of a material).

RADIOACTIVE/RADIOACTIVITY The property of some materials that emit radiation or energetic particles from the nucleus of their atoms.

RADIOACTIVE DECAY The change that takes place inside radioactive materials and causes them to give out progressively less radiation over time.

RADIO GALAXY A galaxy that gives out radio waves of enormous power.

RADIO INTERFERENCE Reduction in the radio communication effectiveness of the ionosphere caused by sunspots and other increases in the solar wind.

RADIO TELESCOPE A telescope that is designed to detect radio waves rather than light waves.

RADIO WAVES A form of electromagnetic radiation, like light and heat. Radio waves have a longer wavelength than light waves.

RADIUS (pl. **RADII**) The distance from the center to the outside of a circle or sphere.

RAY A line across the surface of a planet or moon made by material from a crater being flung across the surface.

REACTION An opposition to a force.

REACTIVE The ability of a chemical substance to combine readily with other substances. Oxygen is an example of a reactive substance.

RED GIANT A cool, large, bright star at least 25 times the diameter of our Sun.

REFLECT/REFLECTION/REFLECTIVE To bounce back any light that falls on a surface.

REGULAR SATELLITES Satellites that orbit in the same direction as their parent planet. This motion is also called synchronous rotation.

RESOLVING POWER The ability of an optical telescope to form an image of a distant object.

RETROGRADE DIRECTION An orbit the opposite of normal—that is, a planet that spins so the Sun rises in the west and sinks in the east.

RETROROCKET A rocket that fires against the direction of travel in order to slow down a space vehicle.

RIDGE A narrow crest of an upland area.

RIFT A trench made by the sinking of a part of the crust between parallel faults.

RIFT VALLEY A long trench in the surface of a planet produced by the collapse of the crust in a narrow zone.

ROCKET Any kind of device that uses the principle of jet propulsion, that is, the rapid release of gases designed to propel an object rapidly.

The word is also applied loosely to fireworks and spacecraft launch vehicles.

ROCKET ENGINE A propulsion system that burns liquid fuel such as liquid hydrogen.

ROCKET MOTOR A propulsion system that burns solid fuel such as hydrazine.

ROCKETRY Experimentation with rockets.

ROTATION Spinning around an axis.

SAND DUNE An aerodynamically shaped hump of sand.

SAROS CYCLE The interval of 18 years $11^1/_3$ days needed for the Earth, Sun, and Moon to come back into the same relative positions. It controls the pattern of eclipses.

SATELLITE (1) An object that is in an orbit around another object, usually a planet.

The Moon is a satellite of the Earth.

See also: **IRREGULAR SATELLITE, MOON, GALILEAN SATELLITE, REGULAR SATELLITE, SHEPHERD SATELLITE.**

(2) A man-made object that orbits the Earth. Usually used as a term for an unmanned spacecraft whose job is to acquire or transfer data to and from the ground.

SATURN The sixth planet from the Sun and three planets farther away from the Sun than the Earth.

It is the least-dense planet in the solar system, having 95 times the mass of the Earth, but 766 times the volume. It is one of the gas giant planets.

SCARP The steep slope of a sharp-crested ridge.

SEASONS The characteristic cycle of events in the heating of the Earth that causes related changes in weather patterns.

SEDIMENT Any particles of material that settle out, usually in layers, from a moving fluid such as air or water.

SEDIMENTARY Rocks deposited in layers.

SEISMIC Shaking, relating to earthquakes.

SENSOR A device used to detect something. Your eyes, ears, and nose are all sensors. Satellites use sensors that mainly detect changes in radio and other waves, including sunlight.

SHEPHERD SATELLITES Larger natural satellites that have an influence on small debris in nearby rings because of their gravity.

SHIELD VOLCANO A volcanic cone that is broad and gently sloping.

SIDEREAL MONTH The average time that the Moon takes to return to the same position against the background of stars.

SILT Particles with a range of 2 microns to 60 microns across.

SLINGSHOT TRAJECTORY A path chosen to use the attractive force of gravity to increase the speed of a spacecraft.

The craft is flown toward the planet or star, and it speeds up under the gravitational force. At the correct moment the path is taken to send the spacecraft into orbit and, when pointing in the right direction, to turn it from orbit, with its increased velocity, toward the final destination.

SOLAR Anything to do with the Sun.

SOLAR CELL A photoelectric device that converts the energy from the Sun (solar radiation) into electrical energy.

SOLAR FLARE Any sudden explosion from the surface of the Sun that sends ultraviolet radiation into the chromosphere. It also sends out some particles that reach Earth and disrupt radio communications.

SOLAR PANELS Large flat surfaces covered with thousands of small photoelectric devices that convert solar radiation into electricity.

SOLAR RADIATION The light and heat energy sent into space from the Sun.

Visible light and heat are just two of the many forms of energy sent by the Sun to the Earth.

SOLAR SYSTEM The Sun and the bodies orbiting around it.

The solar system contains nine major planets, at least 60 moons (large natural satellites), and a vast number of asteroids and comets, together with the gases within the system.

SOLAR WIND The flow of tiny charged particles (called plasma) outward from the Sun.

The solar wind stretches out across the solar system.

SONIC BOOM The noise created when an object moves faster than the speed of sound.

SPACE Everything beyond the Earth's atmosphere.

The word "space" is used rather generally. It can be divided up into inner space—the solar system, and outer space—everything beyond the solar system, for example, interstellar space.

SPACECRAFT Anything capable of moving beyond the Earth's atmosphere. Spacecraft can be manned or unmanned. Unmanned spacecraft are often referred to as space probes if they are exploring new areas.

SPACE RACE The period from the 1950s to the 1970s when the United States and the Soviet Union competed to be first in achievements in space.

SPACE SHUTTLE NASA's reusable space vehicle that is launched like a rocket but returns like a glider.

SPACE STATION A large man-made satellite used as a base for operations in space.

SPEED OF LIGHT *See:* **LIGHT-YEAR.**

SPHERE A ball-shaped object.

SPICULES Jets of relatively cool gas that move upward through the chromosphere into the corona.

SPIRAL GALAXY A galaxy that has a core of stars at the center of long curved arms made of even more stars arranged in a spiral shape.

SPRING TIDE A tide showing the greatest difference between high and low tides.

STAR A large ball of gases that radiates light. The star nearest the Earth is the Sun.

There are enormous numbers of stars in the universe, but few can be seen with the naked eye. Stars may occur singly, as our Sun, or in groups, of which pairs are most common.

STAR CLUSTER A group of gravitationally connected stars.

STELLAR WIND The flow of tiny charged particles (called plasma) outward from a star.

In our solar system the stellar wind is the same as the solar wind.

STRATOSPHERE The region immediately above the troposphere where the temperature increases with height, and the air is always stable.

It acts like an invisible lid, keeping the clouds in the troposphere.

SUBDUCTION ZONES Long, relatively thin, but very deep regions of the crust where one plate moves down and under, or subducts, another. They are the source of mountain ranges.

SUN The star that the planets of the solar system revolve around.

The Sun is 150 million km from the Earth and provides energy (in the form of light and heat) to our planet. Its density of 1.4 grams per cubic centimeter is similar to that of a gas giant planet.

SUNSPOT A spiral of gas found on the Sun that is moving slowly upward, and that is cooler than the surrounding gas and so looks darker.

SUPERNOVA A violently exploding star that becomes millions or even billions of times brighter than when it was younger and stable.

See also: **NOVA.**

SYNCHRONOUS Taking place at the same time.

SYNCHRONOUS ORBIT An orbit in which a satellite (such as a moon) moves around a planet in the same time that it takes for the planet to make one rotation on its axis.

SYNCHRONOUS ROTATION When two bodies make a complete rotation on their axes in the same time.

As a result, each body always has the same side facing the other. The Moon and Venus are in synchronous rotation with the Earth.

SYNODIC MONTH The complete cycle of phases of the Moon as seen from Earth. It is 29.531 solar days (29 days, 12 hours, 44 minutes, 3 seconds).

SYNODIC PERIOD The time needed for an object within the solar system, such as a planet, to return to the same place relative to the Sun as seen from the Earth.

TANGENT A direction at right angles to a line radiating from a circle or sphere.

If you make a wheel spin, for example, by repeatedly giving it a glancing blow with your hand, the glancing blow is moving along a tangent.

TELECOMMUNICATIONS Sending messages by means of telemetry, using signals made into waves such as radio waves.

THEORY OF RELATIVITY A theory based on how physical laws change when an observer is moving. Its most famous equation says that at the speed of light, energy is related to mass and the speed of light.

THERMOSPHERE A region of the upper atmosphere above the mesosphere.

It absorbs ultraviolet radiation and is where the ionosphere has most effect.

THRUST A very strong and continued pressure.

THRUSTER A term for a small rocket engine.

TIDE Any kind of regular, or cyclic, change that occurs due to the effect of the gravity of one body on another.

We are used to the ocean waters of the Earth being affected by the gravitational pull of the Moon, but tides also cause a small alteration of the shape of a body. This is important in determining the shape of many moons and may even be a source of heating in some.

See also: **NEAP TIDE** and **SPRING TIDE.**

TOPOGRAPHY The shape of the land surface in terms of height.

TOTAL ECLIPSE When one body (such as the Moon or Earth) completely obscures the light source from another body (such as the Earth or Moon).

A total eclipse of the Sun occurs when it is completely blocked out by the Moon.

A total eclipse of the Moon occurs when it passes into the Earth's shadow to such a degree that light from the Sun is completely blocked out.

TRAJECTORY The curved path followed by a projectile.

See also: **SLINGSHOT TRAJECTORY.**

TRANSPONDER Wireless receiver and transmitter.

TROPOSPHERE The lowest region of the atmosphere, where all of the Earth's clouds form.

TRUSS Tubing arrayed in the form of triangles and designed to make a strong frame.

ULTRAVIOLET A form of radiation that is just beyond the violet end of the visible spectrum and so is called "ultra" (more than) violet. At the other end of the visible spectrum is "infra" (less than) red.

UMBRA (1) A region that is in complete darkness during an eclipse.

(2) The darkest region in the center of a sunspot.

UNIVERSE The entirety of everything there is; the cosmos.

Many space scientists prefer to use the term "cosmos," referring to the entirety of energy and matter.

UNSTABLE In atmospheric terms the potential churning of the air in the atmosphere as a result of air being heated from below. There is a chance of the warmed, less-dense air rising through the overlying colder, more-dense air.

UPLINK A communication from Earth to a spacecraft.

URANUS The seventh planet from the Sun and four planets farther from the Sun than the Earth.

Its diameter is four times that of the Earth. It is one of the gas giant planets.

VACUUM A space that is entirely empty.

A vacuum lacks any matter.

VALLEY A natural long depression in the landscape.

VELOCITY A more precise word to describe how something is moving, because movement has both a magnitude (speed) and a direction.

VENT The tube or fissure that allows volcanic materials to reach the surface of a planet.

VENUS The second planet from the Sun and our closest neighbor.

It appears as an evening and morning "star" in the sky. Venus is very similar to the Earth in size and mass.

VOLCANO A mound or mountain that is formed from ash or lava.

VOYAGER A pair of U.S. space probes designed to provide detailed information about the outer regions of the solar system.

Voyager 1 was launched on September 5, 1977. Voyager 2 was launched on August 20, 1977, but traveled more slowly than Voyager 1. Both Voyagers are expected to remain operational until 2020, by which time they will be well outside the solar system.

WATER CYCLE The continuous cycling of water, as vapor, liquid, and solid, between the oceans, the atmosphere, and the land.

WATER VAPOR The gaseous form of water. Also sometimes referred to as moisture.

WEATHERING The breaking down of a rock, perhaps by water, ice, or repeated heating and cooling.

WHITE DWARF Any star originally of low mass that has reached the end of its life.

X-RAY An invisible form of radiation that has extremely short wavelengths just beyond the ultraviolet.

X-rays can go through many materials that light will not.

SET INDEX

Using the set index

This index covers all eight volumes in the *Space Science* set:

Vol. no.	Title
1:	*How the universe works*
2:	*Sun and solar system*
3:	*Earth and Moon*
4:	*Rocky planets*
5:	*Gas giants*
6:	*Journey into space*
7:	*Shuttle to Space Station*
8:	*What satellites see*

An example entry:
Index entries are listed alphabetically.

Moon rover **3:** 48–49, **6:** 51

Volume numbers are in bold and are followed by page references.

In the example above, "Moon rover" appears in Volume 3: *Earth and Moon* on pages 48–49 and in Volume 6: *Journey into space* on page 51. Many terms are also covered separately in the Glossary on pages 58–64.

See, see also, or *see under* refers to another entry where there will be additional relevant information.